CHRIST
IN
ISLAM

by James Robson
Foreword by Andrew Phillip Smith

Also Available from Bardic Press

Boyhood With Gurdjieff; Gurdjieff Remembered; Balanced Man
by Fritz Peters (not available in the USA)

New Nightingale, New Rose:
Poems From the Divan of Hafiz
translated by Richard Le Gallienne

The Quatrains of Omar Khayyam:
Three Translations of the Rubaiyat
*translated by Edward Fitzgerald, Justin McCarthy
and Richard Le Gallienne*

The Gospel of Thomas and Christian Wisdom
Stevan Davies

Celtic Folklore: Welsh and Manx
John Rhys

Don't Forget: P.D. Ouspensky's Life of Self-remembering
Bob Hunter

The Life, Work and Teaching of Rodney Collin
Andrew Phillip Smith

The Door of the Beloved: Poems of Hafiz
Justin McCarthy

**Visit our website at www.bardic-press.com
email us at info@bardic-press.com**

CHRIST IN ISLAM

by James Robson
Foreword by Andrew Phillip Smith

Bardic Press
California 2006

Copyright © 2006 Bardic Press
Foreword Copyright © 2006 Andrew Phillip Smith

Printed on acid-free paper

Published by Bardic Press
PO Box 761
Oregon House
CA 95962
USA

http://www.bardic-press.com
info@bardic-press.com

Contents

Foreword

Introduction   7

Chapter 1: Passages from the Koran   17
Chapter 2: Traditional Stories   29
Chapter 3: Moral and Religious Sayings   42
Chapter 4: Ascetic Sayings   63
Chapter 5: Sayings of God to Jesus   78
Chapter 6: Miscellaneous Passages   81
Chapter 7: Stories Connected with Jesus   95

Foreword

According to the Islamic religion, Jesus was the last great prophet before Muhammad. His status within Islam is confirmed by the large body of sayings attributed to Jesus, and teaching stories in which Jesus plays an important part. These tales and aphorisms are spread throughout the literature, from the Qur'an to the Sufi poets and the great Muslim philosophers. This extensive tradition has unfortunately remained largely unknown to the western Christian tradition.

Until recently, James Robson's *Christ in Islām* was the fullest and most accessible collection of material. It is still consistently referenced in the bibliographies of scholarly books, yet it has been out of print for several decades. Tarif Khalidi's *The Muslim Jesus* has supplanted Robson's book as a scholarly collection of sayings, but *Christ in Islam* contains stories and sayings, and passages from the Qur'an, which were excluded from Khalidi's excellent collection. Thus, Robson's book is still unique.

James Robson's translations are clear and unfussy, and preserve the pithiness of these aphorisms and stories. His chapter themes are somewhat unhelpful, but they at least allow us to perceive some of the characteristics of the figure of Jesus in the Muslim material.

Anyone who encounters these traditions for the first time is bound to ask where they ultimately come from, and to what extent they are authentic. As I show in my book *The Lost Sayings of Jesus: Annotated & Explained* (Skylight Paths, 2006), there is an extensive tradition of the sayings of Jesus outside of the canonical gospels, which survives mainly in apocryphal gospels and the Gnostic material, in quotation from church fathers, and in the Islamic tradition. While the majority of these were probably never spoken by Jesus, we ought to remember that we do not actually know which of the the sayings of Jesus contained in the New Testament were spoken by him either, and modern scholarship has grown increasingly skeptical of being able to unequivocally attribute the origin of a saying to Jesus himself. The same is true of the Muslim tradition, especially since many of the texts in which the sayings and stories are to be found were written down well over a millennium after the death of Jesus.

Yet it is not unlikely that some of these sayings might have been preserved in the Christian manuscript tradition, and hence made their way into Muslim culture. Islām considered itself to be the successor to Judaism and Christianity, and

Muhammad certainly knew Jews and Christians and learned from them. The stories in Qur'an in which Mary gives birth to Jesus beneath a palm tree, and in which Jesus makes birds out of clay are also found in the apocryphal infancy gospels. The Qur'anic view that Jesus was not actually crucified, is also found in the Gnostic text, *The Second Treatise of The Great Seth*. If these noncanonical stories were known to Muhammad, noncanonical sayigs might also have been transmitted to him. As Islām developed, Muslim scholars were eager to learn from the writings of Jews and Christians, "people of the book", along with the writings of the pagan Greek-speaking world. It is certainly not impossible that sayings of Jesus preserved in, for instance, Syrian Christian texts, might have been preserved longer in the Muslim world than they were in the Christian cultures. Many of the sayings found in al-Ghazali's *Revival of the Religious Sciences*, a major source for Robson's material, may come from a sayings collection similar to the Gospel of Thomas, as Robert M. Price has suggested in *Deconstructing Jesus*.

But regardless of their ultimate origin, these tales and aphorisms sparkle by themselves, like gemstones removed from the rings which house them. The Muslim Jesus has his own character. He is hard on himself and his body, and wedded to poverty, as the section entitled Ascetic Sayings indicates. He is a wander, like many of the sufis.

Sometimes he is referred to as the messiah, a title that does not have the same implication in Muslim theology as it does in the Christian, yet he is a humble man. He is eager to learn from the chance events and encounters of his life, yet he is also a stern teacher. Parables are few, but the miraculous is always just around the corner. The consistent tone of the Islamic accounts of Jesus helps to create an alternative Jesus who in his way is just as real as the Jesus of the New Testament gospels, and as profound.

ANDREW PHILLIP SMITH

Introduction

WHEN Mohammad established Islām in Arabia he insisted that he was not proclaiming a new religion, for he believed that all the prophets who preceded him had brought the same message. From time to time God had sent prophets and had revealed His will in sacred books; but men were rebellious, and so it was necessary for Him periodically to send a new prophet to lead them back to the truth. Mohammad had no sense of any gradual development in the knowledge of God, for he held that a knowledge of the true religion had been given to man from the beginning. The reason why God needed to send prophets with fresh revelations was because men had fallen away from the truth and required to be called back to it. Thus men like Abraham, Moses, Jesus, and himself had all the same task set before them, and none of them was essentially different from any other. God might authorise one to abrogate certain practices which had been commanded by a predecessor, but in essential matters they were all engaged in the same task, which was to proclaim the unity of God and summon men to worship Him alone.

Christ in Islam

This being Mohammad's belief, it naturally follows that he was unable to accept what Christians taught regarding the person of Jesus. To him Jesus was no more than a prophet, even though He is accorded a dignity which is given to no other. The Korān speaks of the Virgin Birth; calls Jesus God's Word and a spirit from Him; declares that He is "eminent in this world and the next, and one of those who approach God's presence;" and attributes wonderful miracles to Him. But Mohammad could not admit that He was anything more than other men. He understood the doctrine of His Sonship in a carnal sense, and therefore he very naturally denied it vigorously. As an example of the Muslim rejection of this doctrine, one might quote the argument of Abū 'Othman 'Amr Ibn Bahr al Jāhiz, who lived in the ninth century of our era. He said that if God is a Father, He must also be a grandfather and an uncle; and insisted that the birth of Jesus was not so unique as that of Adam and Eve, for they had neither father nor mother.

The purpose of this volume is to present an account of Jesus as He appears in the works of Muslim writers. I have collected the relevant passages from the Korān, of which I give my own translation, and I hope that it will not be found that I have inadvertently omitted any. I have confined myself to those passages which

Christ in Islam

make a definite reference to Jesus, omitting those which are merely directed towards Christians with no particular reference to Jesus. No attempt has been made to arrange these passages so as to give a chronological account of the life and teaching of Jesus; they are presented in the order in which they occur in the Korān. I have added a few selections from Tha'labī's Kisas al Anbiyā' (Stories of the Prophets), along with one passage from Abū al Fidā's Universal History. The ultimate source of this latter work is Tabarī's history, but I have chosen Abū al Fidā's account rather than Tabari's because it is shorter.

The main part of this volume consists of sayings attributed to Jesus and stories about Him which are found in the writings of various Muslim writers. Professor Margoliouth collected 77 passages, 71 of which are from Ghazālī's Ihyā' 'Ulūm ad Dīn (Revival of the Religious Sciences), and 6 from other sources. These were published in five parts in vol. v of the Expository Times (1893-4). Michaël Asin y Palacios, the professor of Arabic in Madrid University, has published a work in two parts, entitled Logia et Agrapha nomini Jesu apud Moslemicos Scriptores, asceticos præsertim, usitata, which contains 233 passages. It is published in Patrologia Orientalis, vols. xiii and xix. The first volume deals with Ghazālī's work referred to above, with the addition of parallel passages from other writers; and the second consists of passages from various writers. Margoliouth's collection gives a translation of the passages with occasional explanatory notes; Asin gives the Arabic text of all but the last eight passages, with a Latin translation and notes in Latin. Asin includes some passages which refer to John the Baptist, Zechariah, and Mary which I have not translated, as they do not come within the purpose of this book. I have also omitted variants and the passages of which the Arabic text is not given. In both these collections the passages are given in the order in which they occur in the sources from which they are taken, but I have not followed this order. For the sake of showing various aspects of the Muslim representation of Jesus, I have attempted to group the passages under several headings.

Both collections number the passages, so I have indicated the numbers for the benefit of those who care to refer to them. To save space, "A." is used for Asin's collection, and "M." for Margoliouth's. References are also given to the other passages. The numbers of the surahs and the verses in the Korān are given. "Th." stands for Thaʿlabī's stories, the pages to which reference is made being those in the edition which I used, that printed in Cairo in 1310 A.H. (1892 A.D.). "A.F." stands for Abū al Fidā, the edition

Christ in Islam

referred to being Fleischer's, published in Leipzig in 1831.

In the passages which are translated in this volume it will be seen that Jesus is treated as merely a prophet and teacher, who is not necessarily better than other pious people. One should beware of laying too much stress on the title "Spirit of God" by which He is frequently addressed, for this is merely an echo of words used in the Korān. He is represented as feeling Himself less worthy to pray for rain than a man who had plucked out his eye because it had looked at a woman (A. 10, p. 95); He is described as being gloomy in contrast to John the Baptist, who was cheerful, and whom God commends as being the more attractive (A. 121, p. 108); He is rebuked by God for failing to understand the piety of a simple man (A. 208, p. 125); He takes warning when He finds that Satan has discovered some evil in Him (A. 174 bis, p. 76). All this is quite in keeping with the Muslim conception of His person; but it naturally raises a question as to whether there can be any element of genuineness in such passages.

The problem of determining the origin of the sayings and stories is a difficult one. In some instances it is obvious that the writer had access to the New Testament, or more probably had a second-hand knowledge of it, and so made a fairly accurate quotation, e.g. A. 55, p. 46, A. 65, p. 47.

Christ in Islam

In dealing with other sayings one hesitates to pronounce an opinion as to their genuineness or otherwise. It is important to notice that Asin is convinced that some of the sayings are genuine, although he does not commit himself absolutely to this position. When he comes to a saying which he feels is genuine, his favourite phrase is "Agraphum mihi videtur." The Rev. R. Dunkerley published two excellent articles in the Expository Times of January and February 1928, on "The Muhammadan Agrapha," in which he is inclined to support Asin's feeling that some sayings are genuine; and he gives four reasons for doing so. (1) It is reasonable to expect that unrecorded sayings of Jesus had long been cherished in out-of-the-way parts of Arabia and Mesopotamia. (2) When the ascription to Jesus is definite, unchallenged, and of early date, and when several witnesses agree, there are grounds for holding a saying to be genuine. (3) If a passage contains teaching alien to or opposed to Islām it may be taken as coming from a Christian source. (4) If a saying has the aptness and precision characteristic of Gospel sayings, we may be disposed to accept it. These are sound principles of judgment, but there must always be a doubt.

In many instances, however, one need have little doubt about rejecting the genuineness of passages. The wonderful stories of the raising of the

Christ in Islam

dead, a speaking skull, etc., are obvious fictions. Such a story as A. 148, p. 114, which speaks of a mountain bewailing the fact that idols had been hewn from it, is clearly of Muslim origin, as it is based on some words from the Korān. But A. 215, p. 93, is strange, for while it quotes words which are attributed to Jesus in the Korān, it adds to them something which would seem to have a Christian origin.

The large number of ascetic passages may surprise some readers, but one must remember that the Nestorian Church in Mesopotamia laid great emphasis on asceticism, and that many of their monks secluded themselves in the deserts of Arabia. It may well be that one source of these sayings is to be found in this region. Another point to note is that there is a greater element of asceticism in the sayings of Jesus recorded in the New Testament than one commonly recognises. But even allowing for these considerations, one cannot help feeling that a great amount of this group of sayings is the growth of a later age when asceticism was regarded by many as necessary for salvation.

As regards Thaʻlabī's stories, and also some passages in the Korān, one is able to suggest an origin for some of them in apocryphal Gospels. For example, the story of Jesus being sent to learn the trade of dyeing has a parallel in the Gospel of Thomas, where He is said to have accompanied Mary on a visit to a dyer. The same Gospel has a story in which Jesus changed some children into goats, which suggests an origin for Tha'labī's story of their being changed into swine. There is a passage in the Book of James, or Protevangelium, which speaks of the priests using rods to see who should have charge of Mary, which corresponds to the Korānic story. In the same book Mary is rebuked for unchastity, but this differs from the Korānic passage in that it speaks of this as happening before the birth of Jesus. The Korān speaks of Jesus making a bird of clay, while the Gospel of Thomas speaks of His having made twelve sparrows of clay. The Gospel of Pseudo-Matthew says that when Mary was on her way to Egypt, a palm-tree bowed down to let her pluck its fruit and a spring burst forth, which is reminiscent of the Korānic story where, before the birth of Jesus, a streamlet appears and Mary is told that if she shakes the trunk of a palm-tree it will drop fresh dates. The Gospels of Thomas and of Pseudo-Matthew have also a story similar to that found in A. 206, p. 92. These are only a few parallels which have come to my notice, but they suggest that many of the sayings and stories may have come through Christian channels, and have been accepted in good faith by Muslims, although such as the above are clearly apocryphal. But this indicates that

Christ in Islam

even if a Christian source can be found for many of the passages, it does not necessarily follow that they give us genuine words of Jesus or genuine stories about him.

E. J. Jenkinson, in an article on "Jesus in Moslem Tradition" in the Moslem World of July 1928, gives a parallel from Jewish tradition of Tha'labī's story of the blind man and the lame man, which raises the question as to whether some of the passages are not to be attributed to Jewish sources; and in this connection it is interesting to note that Asin has here and there indicated that sayings which are attributed to Jesus are reminiscent of passages in the Old Testament. And again, it is not unlikely that certain aphorisms or moral stories which had come down for generations were attached to Jesus, although originally they had no connection with Him.

While this discussion necessarily deals very indefinitely with the question of origins, it should be pointed out that Muslims had ample opportunity of coming into contact with Christians from whom they may well have learned some of their traditions. In the time of Mohammad Arabia was surrounded by a number of Christian communities. From Mesopotamia and Syria Christianity extended to the peoples of Hira and Ghassān in North Arabia, and to some of the tribes of the neighbourhood. In the south

Christ in Islam

Christianity had long been represented; and about the time of Mohammad's birth an attempt was made to divert the worship of the Arabs from the kaʻba in Mecca to a Christian church which had been built in Sanʻāʼ in the Yemen; but the expedition was a failure. In Nejrān there was a Christian church which had undergone severe persecution not long before this.

When Islām gained in strength, members of Christian tribes were gradually absorbed into the new religion, and before long Christianity was wiped out of Arabia. But as the conquests extended beyond the bounds of Arabia the Muslims came into contact with other Christian communities. Christians were given the alternative of accepting Islām or paying tribute; and while many adopted Islām, many others retained their religion. The Christians were commonly given very fair treatment, and, especially in the early days, many of them were employed in Government offices.

Thus the Muslim community had in its midst two groups from whom it was possible to gather information regarding Jesus: the Christian communities and converts from Christianity to Islām.

Note.—In addition to the passages mentioned on p. 10, it has been found necessary to omit A. 218, 219, 224 owing to considerations of space.

Chapter 1
Passages From the Korān

II, 81.—And We have brought Moses the Book and sent the apostles after him. And We have brought Jesus, son of Mary, the proofs, and strengthened him with the Holy Spirit.

II, 254.—And We brought Jesus, son of Mary, the proofs, and strengthened him with the Holy Spirit.

III, 31.—When the wife of 'Imrān said, "My Lord, verily I have vowed to Thee that which is in my womb, dedicated [to Thee], so accept [it] from me; verily Thou art He who hears and knows." Then when she gave birth she said, "My Lord, verily I have given birth to a female" (and God knew well what she had given birth to); "and a male is not like a female; and verily I have called her Mary, and verily I commend her and her offspring to Thy protection from the accursed Satan."

III, 37-52.—And when the angels said, "O Mary, verily God has chosen you and purified

Christ in Islam

you and chosen you above the women of the worlds. O Mary, obey your Lord, and worship and bow down with those who bow down." That is one of the pieces of information regarding the unseen which We reveal to you, although you were not with them when they were casting their reeds [to see] which of them should have charge of Mary, and were not with them when they were disputing. When the angels said, "O Mary, verily God gives you good news of a Word from Him, whose name shall be the Messiah, Jesus, son of Mary, eminent in this world and the next, and one of those who approach God's presence. And he shall speak to men in the cradle and when he is grown up, and shall be one of the upright." She said, "My Lord, how can I have a son when no man has touched me?" He said, "Thus God creates what He wills; when He decrees a thing, He only says to it, 'Be,' and it comes into being. And He will teach him the Book, and wisdom, and the Pentateuch, and the Gospel; and [will appoint him] an apostle to the Children of Israel, [saying], 'I have brought you a sign from your Lord. Verily I will create for you of clay something like a bird and will blow into it, and it will become a bird by God's permission; and I will cure the blind from birth and the leper, and will raise the dead by God's permission, and will inform you about what you shall eat and what

Christ in Islam

you shall store up in your houses. Verily in that is a sign for you, if you are believers. And [I come] confirming what is before me with respect to the Pentateuch, and to make lawful for you some of that which has been forbidden you. And I have brought you a sign from your Lord; so fear God and obey me. Verily God is my Lord and your Lord, so worship Him; this is a straight path.'" But when Jesus perceived their unbelief he said, "Who will be my helpers towards God?" The disciples said, "We will be God's helpers; we believe in God and witness that we are Muslims. O our Lord, we believe in what Thou hast sent down, and we have followed the apostle; so write us down with those who bear witness." And they plotted, but God plotted, and God is the best of plotters. When God said, "O Jesus, verily I will cause you to die, and will raise you to Myself, and will cleanse you from those who are unbelievers, and will put those who followed you above those who were unbelievers until the Day of Resurrection; then to Me will be your return. [*This last phrase is not addressed to Jesus, as the pronoun is plural.*] And I will judge between you about that in which you disagree. Then as regards those who were unbelievers, I will punish them severely in this world and the next, and they shall have no helpers." And as regards those who believed and did good deeds, He will pay them their rewards, for God does not love the unjust. That do We recite to you of the signs and the wise reminder. Verily Jesus in the sight of God is like Adam whom He created of earth, then said to him, "Be," and he came into being.

IV, 154-157.—Because of their unbelief and their speaking great slander against Mary, and their saying, "Verily we have killed the Messiah, Jesus, son of Mary, God's apostle." But they did not kill him, and they did not crucify him, but one was made to appear to them like him. And verily those who disagreed about him are in doubt regarding him; they have no knowledge of him but the following of opinion, and they did not really kill him. On the contrary, God raised him to Himself; and God is mighty and wise. And there shall not be any of the people of the Book who will not believe in him before his death; and on the Day of Resurrection he will be a witness against them.

IV, 169, 170.—O people of the Book, do not be fanatical in your religion, and do not say anything but the truth about God. The Messiah, Jesus, son of Mary, is only God's apostle and His Word which He cast into Mary, and a spirit from Him. So believe in God and His apostles, and do not say, "[He is] three." Abstain, and it will be better for you. God is only one God. Far be it from Him that He should have a son!

Christ in Islam

What is in the heavens and what is in the earth are His, and God suffices as Governor. The Messiah does not scorn to be a servant of God, nor do the angels who are near His presence. All those who scorn His worship and are proud will He gather to Himself.

V, 19.—They have disbelieved who said, "Verily God is the Messiah, son of Mary." Say, "Who could prevent God at all if He wished to destroy the Messiah, son of Mary, and his mother, and all who are in the earth?"

V, 50, 51, [following on reference to previous prophets].—And we made Jesus, son of Mary, follow in their traces, verifying what was before him respecting the Pentateuch; and we brought him the Gospel in which is guidance and light; and [he was] verifying what was before him with respect to the Pentateuch, and was a guidance and warning to the God-fearing. And let the people of the Gospel judge by what God has sent down in it; but whoever does not judge by what God has sent down, those are the impious.

V, 76-79.—They have disbelieved who said, "Verily God is the Messiah, son of Mary," when the Messiah said, "O Children of Israel, worship God, my Lord and your Lord." Verily he who takes a partner to God, God has forbidden Paradise to him, and his destination will be hell, and the unjust will have no helpers. They have disbelieved who said, "Verily God is the third

Christ in Islam

of three," when there is no God but one God; and if they do not abstain from what they say, a painful punishment will befall those of them who disbelieved. Will they not turn to God in repentance and ask His pardon? For God is forgiving and compassionate. The Messiah, son of Mary, was only an apostle—the apostles have passed away before him—and his mother was an upright woman; they were both eating food.

V, 82.—Those of the Children of Israel who disbelieved were cursed by the tongue of David and of Jesus, son of Mary. That was because they were disobedient and were transgressors.

V, 109-118.—When God said, "O Jesus, son of Mary, remember my favour to you and to your mother when I strengthened you by the Holy Spirit; you were speaking to men in the cradle and when grown up; and when I taught you the Book and wisdom, and the Pentateuch and the Gospel; and when you were creating from clay something like a bird by My permission and were blowing into it and it was becoming a bird by My permission; and you were curing the blind from birth and the leper by My permission; and when you were raising the dead by My permission; and when I turned away the Children of Israel from you when you brought them the proofs, then those of them who disbelieved said, 'This is nothing but clear magic;' and when I revealed to the disciples, 'Believe

Christ in Islam

in Me and My apostles,' they said, 'We believe and witness that we are Muslims.'"

When the disciples said, "O Jesus, son of Mary, is your Lord able to send down to us a table from heaven?" he said, "Fear God if you are believers." They said, "We wish to eat of it that our hearts may be at rest, and that we may know that you have spoken the truth to us, and that we may be witnesses to it." Jesus, son of Mary, said, "O God our Lord, send down to us a table from heaven which will be a feast for us, for the first of us and the last of us, and a sign from Thee. And give us provision, for Thou art the best of providers." God said, "Verily I am sending it down to you, so whoever of you disbelieves afterwards, I will punish him in a way in which I will not punish anyone in the worlds."

And when God said, "O Jesus, son of Mary, did you say to men, 'Take me and my mother as gods besides God?'" he said, "Praise be to God! It is not fitting for me to say what is not mine by right. If I had said it Thou wouldest have known it; Thou knowest what is in my soul, but I do not know what is in Thy soul; verily Thou art the Knower of hidden things. I said to them only what Thou commanddest me, 'Worship God, my Lord and your Lord,' and I was a witness against them as long as I was among them. If Thou punishest them, they are Thy servants; and if Thou forgivest them, Thou art the mighty and the wise One."

VI, 84-90.—And We gave him [Abraham] Isaac and Jacob, both We guided, and Noah We guided formerly; and of his seed were David and Solomon and Job and Joseph and Moses and Aaron, and thus do We reward those who do good; and Zechariah and John and Jesus and Elijah, all were of the upright; and Ishmael and Elisha and Jonah and Lot, and we favoured them all above the worlds; and some of their fathers and offspring and brethren, and We chose them and guided them to a straight path. That is God's guidance with which He guides those of His servants whom He wills; but if they had been idolaters, what they were doing would have been fruitless. Those were they to whom We brought the Book and authority and prophecy; so if these disbelieve in it, We will put it in trust of a people who will not disbelieve in it. Those are they whom God guides, so follow their guidance.

IX, 30-32.—The Jews said, "Ezra is the son of God;" and the Christians said, "The Messiah is the son of God." That is their saying with their mouths. They imitate what former disbelievers said. God fight with them! How are they turned away! They have taken their doctors and monks as lords besides God, and the Messiah, son of Mary, when they were commanded to worship only one God. There is

Christ in Islam

no God but He. Far be He from what they associate with Him! They wish to extinguish God's light with their mouths, and God refuses but to perfect His light, even if the unbelievers dislike it.

XIX, 16-34.—And mention in the Book Mary, when she withdrew from her people in an eastern place and took a veil apart from them. Then We sent Our spirit to her, and he appeared to her as a well-formed man. She said, "Verily I take refuge in the Merciful from you if you are God-fearing." He replied, "I am only the messenger of your Lord to give you a pure boy." She said, "How can I have a boy when no man has touched me, and I am not a prostitute?" He replied, "Thus has your Lord said, 'It is easy for Me, and We will make him a sign to men and a mercy from Us, and it is a matter that is decreed.'" Then she conceived him and withdrew with him to a remote place; and the pangs of childbirth made her come to the trunk of a palm-tree. She said, "Would that I had died before this and had been forgotten and unremembered!" Then he called to her from under her, "Do not grieve; your Lord has put a streamlet below you; and shake towards you the trunk of the palm-tree, and it will let fresh, ripe dates fall on you; so eat and drink and refresh yourself. And if you see anyone, say, 'Verily I have vowed a fast to the Merciful, so I will not speak to a human being to-day.'" Then she brought him to her people, carrying him. They said, "O Mary, you have brought an extraordinary thing. O sister of Aaron, your father was not a bad man and your mother was not a prostitute." Then she pointed to him. They said, "How can we speak to one who is a boy in the cradle?" He said, "Verily I am God's servant. He has brought me the Book and has made me a prophet and made me blessed wherever I am, and has enjoined on me prayer and alms as long as I live and filial piety to my mother, and He has not made me proud and miserable. And peace be upon me the day I was born and the day I die and the day I am raised up alive!" This is Jesus, son of Mary, the Word of truth, about whom they doubt. It was not fitting for God that He should beget any son. Praise be to Him! When He decrees anything, He only says to it, "Be," and it comes into being.

XXI, 91.—And [remember] her who preserved her chastity and in whom We breathed of Our spirit, and made her and her son a sign to the worlds.

XXIII, 52.—And We made the son of Mary and his mother a sign, and gave them shelter in a hill possessed of security and running water.

XXXIII, 7.—And [remember] when We received from the prophets their covenant, and from you, and from Noah and Abraham and Moses and Jesus, son of Mary; and We received from them a strong covenant.

XLII, 11.—He has ordained to you with respect to religion what He enjoined on Noah and what We revealed to you, and what We enjoined on Abraham and Moses and Jesus, viz. "Establish the religion, and do not divide concerning it."

XLIII, 57-65.—And when the son of Mary was quoted as an example, behold! your people were turning away from him, and they said, "Are our gods better, or he?" They have only quoted him out of skill in argument; verily they are a quarrelsome people. He is only a servant on whom We bestowed favour and whom We made an example to the Children of Israel. And if We pleased, We could make from among you angels succeeding you in the earth; And verily he is a sign [lit. knowledge] of the [last] hour; so do not doubt it, and follow me. This is a straight path. And let not the devil turn you away; verily he is to you a sure enemy. And when Jesus brought the proofs he said, "I have brought you wisdom, and will make clear to you some of that about which you differ; so fear God and obey me. Verily God is my Lord and your Lord, so worship Him. Verily this is a straight path." Then the parties among them disagreed. So woe to those who did unjustly, because of the punishment of a painful day!

Christ in Islam

LVII, 26, 27.—And We have sent Noah and Abraham and have put in their offspring prophecy and the Book, and some of them were rightly guided, but many of them were impious. Then We caused Our apostles to follow in their traces and We caused Jesus, son of Mary, to follow; and We brought him the Gospel and put gentleness and compassion in the hearts of those who followed him. But as for the monastic state, they invented it. We prescribed for them only desire for the acceptance of God; but they did not observe it as it ought to be observed. So We gave their reward to those of them who believed, but many of them were impious.

LXI, 6.—And when Jesus, son of Mary, said, "O Children of Israel, verily I am God's apostle to you verifying what was before me with respect to the Pentateuch and bringing good news of an apostle who will come after me whose name will be Ahmad." Then when he brought them the I proofs they said, "This is clear magic."

LXI, 14.—O you who believe, be God's helpers, as Jesus, son of Mary, said to the disciples, "Who will be my helpers towards God?" The disciples said, "We will be God's helpers." Then a section of the Children of Israel believed, but a section disbelieved; and God strengthened those who believed against their enemy, and they became conquerors.

Chapter 2
Traditional Stories

Th., p. 243.—Ka'b al Ahbār said: Jesus, son of Mary, was a ruddy man, inclined to white; he did not have long hair, and he never anointed his head. Jesus used to walk barefoot, and he took no house, or adornment, or goods, or clothes, or provision except his day's food. Wherever the sun set he arranged his feet in prayer till the morning came. He was curing the blind from birth and the leper and raising the dead by God's permission and was telling his people what they were eating in their houses and what they were storing up for the morrow [cf. Korān III, 43], and he was walking on the surface of the water in the sea. His head was dishevelled and his face was small; he was an ascetic in the world, longing for the next world and eager for the worship of God. He was a pilgrim in the earth till the Jews sought him and desired to kill him. Then God raised him up to heaven; and God knows best.

Th., pp. 241, 242. [The following is a version of the story of the Wise Men from the East.]—That night people went out repairing to him because of a star which had risen. They had been told formerly in the Book of Daniel that the rising of that star would be one of the signs of him who was to be born. So they went out seeking him, and took with them gold, myrrh, and frankincense. They passed one of the kings of Syria who asked them, "Where are you making for?" and they told him about that. He said, "What is the meaning of the myrrh, gold, and frankincense? Will you present him with these things?" They replied, "Those represent him, because gold is the lord of all goods, similarly this prophet (God bless him and grant him peace!) is the lord of the people of his time; and because what is broken and wounded is put right with myrrh, similarly God will heal by this prophet (God bless him and grant him peace!) all who are infirm and ill; and because the smoke of frankincense and no other smoke enters heaven, similarly God will raise this prophet (God bless him and grant him peace!) and no other prophet of his time to heaven." When they said that to that king he decided to kill him, so he said to them, "Go away, and when you learn where he is, tell me about that, for I wish the same with respect to him as you do." They set off until they came to Mary and gave her (Peace be upon her!) the present that was with them. And they desired to return to that king to tell him where he was, but an angel met them and said to them, "Do not return to him and do not tell him where he is, for he only wanted to kill him." So they went off another way.

Th., pp. 243, 244.—Wahb said: The first sign which the people saw from Jesus was that his mother was living in the house of a village headman in the land of Egypt, to which Joseph the carpenter had brought her when he went with her to Egypt, and the poor used to repair to that headman's house. Some money belonging to that headman was stolen from his treasury, but he did not suspect the poor, and Mary was grieved over the affliction of that headman. When Jesus saw his mother's grief over her host's affliction he said to her, "Mother, do you want me to guide him to his money?" She replied, "Yes, my son." He said, "Tell him to gather the poor for me in his house." So Mary said that to the headman and he gathered the poor for him. When they had collected he went to two of them, one of whom was blind and the other lame, and lifted the lame man on to the blind man's shoulder, and said to him, "Rise up with him." The blind man replied, "I am too weak for that." Jesus said to him, "How were you strong enough for it yesterday?" When they heard him saying that, they beat the blind man till he arose, and when he stood up the lame man reached to the window of the treasury. Then Jesus said to the headman,

Christ in Islam

"Thus they schemed against your property yesterday, because the blind man sought the help of his strength and the lame man of his eyes." Then the blind man and the lame man said, "He has spoken the truth, by God! " and restored all his money to the headman. He took it and put it in his treasury and said, "O Mary, take half of it." She replied, "I was not created for that." The headman said, "Then give it to your son." She replied, "He is greater in rank than I."

Soon after the headman gave a marriage-feast for a son of his. He prepared a feast for him and gathered all the people of Egypt to it and was feeding them for two months. Then when that came to an end some people from Syria visited him, but the headman did not know about them till they arrived, and that day he had no wine. When Jesus saw his concern about that, he entered one of the headman's houses in which were two rows of jars and Jesus passed his hand over their mouths while he was walking by; and every time he passed his hand over a jar it became full of wine, until Jesus came to the last of them. And at that time he was twelve years old.

Another sign. As Sadī said: When Jesus (Peace be upon him!) was in the school, he used to tell the boys what their fathers were doing; and he would say to a boy, "Go [home], for

Christ in Islam

your people have been eating such and such and have prepared [?] such and such for you and they are eating such and such." So the boy would go home to his people and would cry till they gave him that thing. Then they would say to him, "Who told you about this?" and he would say, "Jesus." So they shut away their boys from him and said, "Do not play with this magician." So they gathered them in a house, and Jesus came looking for them. Then they said, "They are not here." He said to them, "Then what is in this house?" They replied, "Swine." He said, "Let them be swine." So when they opened the door for them, lo! they were swine. That spread among the people, and the Children of Israel were troubled about it. So when his mother was afraid concerning him she put him on an ass of hers and went in flight to Egypt.

Th., p. 244.—'Atā' said: When Mary had taken Jesus from the school, she handed him over to various trades, and the last to which she entrusted him was to the dyers; so she handed him over to their chief that he might learn from him. Now the man had various clothes with him, and he had to go on a journey, so he said to Jesus, "You have learned this trade, and I am going on a journey from which I shall not return for ten days. These clothes are of different colours, and I have marked every one of them with the colour with which it is to be dyed, so I want you to be finished with them when I return." Then he went out. Jesus (Peace be upon him!) prepared one receptacle with one colour and put all the clothes in it and said to them, "Be, by God's permission, according to what is expected of you." Then the dyer came, and all the clothes were in one receptacle, so he said, "O Jesus, what have you done?" He replied, "I have finished them." He said, "Where are they?" He replied, "In the receptacle." He said, "All of them?" He replied, "Yes." He said, "How are they all in one receptacle? You have spoiled those clothes." He replied, "Rise and look." So he arose, and Jesus took out a yellow garment and a green garment and a red garment until he had taken them out according to the colours which he desired. Then the dyer began to wonder, and he knew that that was from God (Great and glorious is He!). Then the dyer said to the people, "Come and look at what Jesus (Peace be upon him!) has done." So he and his companions, and they were the disciples, believed on him; and God (Great and glorious is He!) knows best.

Th., p. 245.—His prayer by which he was curing the sick and bringing the dead to life was: O God, Thou art the God of those who are in heaven and of those who are on earth; there is no god in them other than Thee. And Thou art

Christ in Islam

the almighty One of those who are in the heavens and the almighty One of those who are on earth; there is no almighty one in them other than Thee. And Thou art the King of those who are in the heavens and the King of those who are on earth; there is no king in them other than Thee. And Thou art the Judge of those who are in the heavens and of those who are on earth; there is no judge in them other than Thee. Thy power on earth is like Thy power in heaven, and Thy authority on earth is like Thy authority in heaven. I ask Thee by Thy noble names. Verily Thou art omnipotent.

Th., p. 245.—Ibn 'Abbās said: They [the disciples] were fishermen who were catching fish, and Jesus passed them and said to them, "What are you doing?" They replied, "We are catching fish." He said to them, "Will you not come with me that you may catch men?" They replied to him, "How do you mean?" He said, "We will summon men to God." They replied, "And who are you?" He said, "I am Jesus, son of Mary, God's servant and apostle." They asked, "Is any of the prophets above you?" He replied, "Yes, the Arabian prophet." So those men followed him and believed on him and set out with him. As Sadī said: They were sailors. Ibn Artāt said: They were fullers and were called that [Hawārīyūn] because they made clothes white.

Christ in Islam

Ibn Fathawaih told us in his tradition from Mus'ab as follows: The disciples were twelve men who followed Jesus; and when they were hungry they said, "O Spirit of God, we are hungry;" then he would strike the ground with his hand, whether on the plain or on a mountain, and two loaves would appear for each man and they would eat them. And when they were thirsty they said, "O Spirit of God, we are thirsty;" then he would strike the ground with his hand, whether on the plain or on a mountain, and water would appear and they would drink. They said, "O Spirit of God, who is better off than we are? When we wish you feed us, and when we wish you give us drink, and we believe in you and have followed you." He replied, "He is better off than you who works with his hand and eats what he has earned." The narrator said: So they began to make clothes for wages.

Th., p. 246.—It is related that Jesus (Peace be upon him!) passed a monastery in which were two blind men and said, "What are these?" The reply was given to him, "These are people who sought death and blinded themselves with their hands." So he said to them, "What urged you to this?" They replied, "We feared the punishment of death, so we did what you see ourselves." Then he said, "You are the learned and the wise and the monks and the excellent ones. Rub your eyes with your hands and say, 'In the name of God.'" So they did that, and lo! they were both standing seeing.

Th., p. 247.—Al Kalbī said, "Jesus was raising the dead by means of "O Living One! O Eternal One!"

Th., p. 247.—It is related that he went out one day in his wandering accompanied by one of his companions who was a short man who attached himself greatly to Jesus. Then when Jesus came to the sea he said, "In the name of God, with health and certainty;" then he walked on the surface of the water. Then the short man said, "In the name of God, with health and certainty;" and he walked on the surface of the water. Then wonder entered him and he said, "This is Jesus, the Spirit of God, walking on the water, and I am walking on the water." The narrator said: Then he sank in the water and appealed to Jesus, so Jesus reached out to him from the water and took him out and said to him, "What did you say, O short one?" He told him what had pervaded his mind and Jesus said to him, "You have put yourself in a place other than that in which God put you and God abhorred you on account of what you said; so turn to God in repentance for what you said." So the man repented and returned to the rank in which God had placed him. So fear God and do not envy one another.

Christ in Islam

Th., pp. 247, 248.—The imām Abū Mansūr al Khamshāwī told us in his tradition from Ma'ādh, son of Jabal, that the apostle of God—i.e. Mohammad (God bless him and grant him peace!)—said, "If you really knew God you would have learned the knowledge after which there is no ignorance, but no one has ever attained to that." They said, "Not even you, O apostle of God?" He replied, "Not even I." They said, "O apostle of God, it has reached us that Jesus, son of Mary, walked on the water." He said, "Yes, and if he had had more fear and certainty, he would have walked on the air." They said, "O apostle of God, we were not thinking that the apostles came short." He replied, "Verily God (Exalted is He!) has too high a rank for anyone to reach His rank."

A.F., pp. 58-62. [After mentioning the names of the disciples.]—These are they who asked him for the descent of the table. So Jesus asked his Lord (Great and glorious is He!) and He sent down to him a red tray covered with a napkin in which was a broiled fish surrounded by vegetables with the exception of the leek, with salt at its head and vinegar at its tail; and along with it were five loaves on some of which were olives and on the others pomegranates and dates. A great number of people ate of them and they did not diminish; and whenever a diseased person ate of them he was cured. And it was coming down one day and disappearing the next for the space of forty nights.

Ibn Saʿīd said: And when God informed the Messiah that he was going from the world he was disturbed at that, and called the disciples and prepared food for them and said, "Come to me to-night, for I have need of you." Then when they gathered at night, he gave them supper and rose to serve them; and when they had finished eating he began to wash their hands and wipe them with his clothes; but they disdained that, so he said, "Whoever rejects anything of what I do is not one of mine." Then they left him alone until he finished. Then he said, "I have only done this that you should have in me an example of serving one another. And as regards my need of you, it is that you should strive for me in prayer to God that my end may be delayed." But when they wished to do that, God cast sleep on them, so that they were incapable of prayer; and the Messiah began to waken them and rebuke them, but they only increased in sleep and laziness and told him that they were too overcome for that. Then the Messiah said, "Praise be to God! The shepherd is taken away and the sheep are scattered." Afterwards he said to them, "Verily I say unto you, one of you will deny me before the cock crows, and one of you will sell me for a small sum of money and will consume my price." And the Jews had been

Christ in Islam

energetic in searching for him; then one of the disciples came to Herod, the governor of the Jews, and to a company of the Jews and said, "What will you assign me if I guide you to the Messiah?" They assigned him thirty dirhems, and he took them and guided them to him. Then God (Exalted is He!) raised the Messiah to Himself and cast his likeness on him who led them to him.

Ibn al Athīr said in the Kāmil: The learned have differed concerning his death before his being raised up. Some say, "He was raised up and did not die." Others say, "No, God made him die for three hours." Others say, "For seven hours, then He brought him back to life." And those who say this are expounding His saying (Exalted is He!), "Verily I will cause you to die and will raise you to Myself." [Korān III, 48.]

And when the Jews seized the person who had been made to resemble him, they bound him and began to lead him with a rope and say to him, "You were raising the dead. Can you not save yourself from this rope?" And they were spitting in his face and putting thorns on him; and they crucified him on the cross for six hours. Then Joseph the carpenter asked for him from the governor who was over the Jews, whose name was Pilate and whose title was Herod, and buried him in a grave which the aforementioned

Christ in Islam

Joseph had prepared for himself. Then God sent down the Messiah from heaven to his mother, Mary, when she was weeping for him, and he said to her, "Verily God has raised me to Himself and nothing but good has befallen me." And he gave her instructions, and she gathered the disciples to him and he sent them through the earth as messengers from God and he ordered them to convey from him [the message which] God had commanded him. Then God raised him to Himself and the disciples scattered where he commanded them. The Messiah's raising up was three hundred and thirty-six years after Alexander's conquest of Darius.

Al Shahrastānī said: Then four of the disciples, Matthew, Luke, Mark, and John, came together, and each of them collected a Gospel, and the end of the Gospel of Matthew is that the Messiah said, "Verily I have sent you to the nations as my Father sent me to you; so go and summon the nations in the name of the Father and the Son and the Holy Ghost."

Chapter 3
Moral and Religious Sayings

A., 1; *M.*, 7.—Jesus (God bless him and grant him peace!) said, "He who knows and works and teaches, that man shall be called great in the kingdom of heaven."

A., 2; *M.*, 8.—Jesus (Peace be upon him!) said, "How many trees are there, yet all of them do not bear fruit; and how many fruits are there, yet all of them are not good; and how many sciences are there, yet all of them are not useful."

A., 3; *M.*, 9.—Jesus (Peace be upon him!) said, "Do not entrust wisdom to those who are unworthy of it, for you wrong it; and do not withhold it from those who are worthy of it, for you wrong them. Be like a kindly doctor who applies the medicine to the diseased spot. He who entrusts wisdom to those who are unworthy of it is foolish, and he who withholds it from those who are worthy of it does wrong. Verily wisdom has a right and it has people who are worthy of it; so give his right to everyone who possesses a right."

A., 4.—Jesus (Peace be upon him!) said,

Christ in Islam

"Do not hang pearls on the necks of swine for wisdom is better than a pearl, and whoever abhors it is worse than swine."

A., 5; M., 10.—Jesus (Peace be upon him!) said, "Learned men who are evil are like a rock which has fallen at the mouth of a river; it does not drink the water, and it does not let the water flow to the field. Learned men who are evil are like the pipe of a lavatory whose outside is plaster, but whose inside is stench. And they are like graves whose outside is flourishing, but whose inside is dead men's bones."

A., 8.—Jesus (Peace be upon him!) said, "He who acquires knowledge and does not act upon it is like a woman who practises immorality in secret, then becomes pregnant and her pregnancy becomes apparent and she is covered with shame. Thus shall God (Exalted is He!) cover with shame on the Day of Resurrection in the sight of witnesses him who does not act upon his knowledge."

A., 9.—It is written in the Pentateuch and the Gospel, "Do not seek knowledge of what you do not know until you practise what you do know."

A., 15; M., 16.—Jesus (Peace be upon him!) said, "Make yourselves lovable to God by hating the disobedient, and come near to God by keeping away from them, and seek God's favour by being displeased with them." They said, "O Spirit of God, with whom, then, shall we associate?" He said, "Associate with him the sight of whom reminds you of God, whose words increase your works, and whose works make you desire the next world."

A., 16; *M.*, 17.—Jesus (Peace be upon him!) said to the disciples, "How would you act if you saw your brother asleep and the wind had blown his cloak off him?" They said, "We should cover and conceal him." He said, "Nay, you would uncover his nakedness." They said, "God forbid! Who would do this?" Then he said, "One of you hears something about his brother, then adds to it and spreads it with an addition."

A., 19; *M.*, 23.—Someone said to Jesus (Peace be upon him!), "Who trained you?" He said, "No one trained me. I saw the ignorance of the ignorant man to be a blemish, so I avoided it."

A., 23; *M.*, 27.—Jesus (Peace be upon him!) said, "Beware of looking, for it sows desire in the heart, and it is sufficient for seduction."

A., 25; *M.*, 28.—Some people said to Jesus (Peace be upon him!), "Direct us to some work by which we shall enter Paradise." He said, "Never say anything." They said, "We are not able to do that." So he said, "Then never say anything but what is good."

A., 27; *M.*, 30.—Jesus (Peace be upon him!) p.

Christ in Islam

45 said, "If one tells many lies, his beauty departs; and if one quarrels with men, his manliness falls to the ground; and if one has many cares, his body becomes ill; and if one has bad manners, he punishes himself."

A., 28; *M.*, 31.—It is related that a pig passed by Jesus (Peace be upon him!), and he said, "Pass in peace." Then someone said, "O Spirit of God, do you say this to a pig?" He replied, "I dislike accustoming my tongue to evil."

A., 29; *M.*, 33.—Mālik, son of Dīnār, said: Jesus (Peace be upon him) and the disciples with him passed by the carcase of a dog. The disciples said, "What a stench this dog makes!" Then he (Blessing and peace be upon him!) said, "How white are its teeth!"

A., 31.—John [the Baptist] said to Jesus (Peace be upon them!), "What is the fiercest thing?" He replied, "God's anger." He said, "Then what comes next to God's anger?" He replied, "That you should be angry." He said, "Then what makes anger begin, and what makes it increase?" He replied, "Pride and boasting and arrogance and indignation."

A., 32; *M.*, 34.—The Messiah, son of Mary (Blessing and peace be upon him!) passed by a company of the Jews; then they spoke evil to him, but he spoke good to them. Then someone said to him, "Verily they are speaking evil, and you are speaking good." He said, "Everyone spends from what he possesses."

A., 33.—It is said that it is written in the Gospel, "He who asks forgiveness for one who has wronged him routs the devil."

A., 51; M., 53.—Jesus (Peace be upon him!) said, "Seek a great amount of what fire cannot consume." Someone said, "And what is that?" He said, "Kindness."

A., 55.—Jesus the Messiah (God bless him and grant him peace!) said, "When a day comes in which one of you fasts, let him anoint his head and his beard and wipe his lips, that men may not see that he is fasting. And when he gives with his right hand let him hide it from his left hand, and when he prays let him lower the screen of his door, for God will apportion praise as He apportions provision." [Cf. A., 87, p. 48.]

A., 56; M., 55.—The Messiah (Peace be upon him!) said, "Blessed is he whom God teaches His Book, and who does not die proud."

A., 57.—The Messiah (Peace be upon him!) said, "Blessed are the humble in this world; they will be set on high on the Day of Resurrection. Blessed are they who make peace between men in this world; they are those who will inherit Paradise on the Day of Resurrection. Blessed are they whose hearts are purified in this world; they are those who will see God (Exalted is He!) on the Day of Resurrection."

Christ in Islam

A., 59; *M.*, 56.—The Messiah (Peace be upon him!) said, "Verily the seed grows on level ground and does not grow on a rock; similarly wisdom works in the heart of the humble but does not work in the heart of the proud. Do you not see that if one raises his head to the roof it breaks it; but if one bends down [his head] it shades him and covers him?"

A., 62.—The disciples said to the Messiah (Peace be upon him!), "Look at this mosque, how beautiful it is!" Then he said, "My people, my people, verily I say unto you, God will not leave one stone of this mosque standing on another, but will destroy it for the sins of its people. Verily God does not pay any heed to gold, or silver, or these stones which charm you. The things dearest to God (Exalted is He!) are the pure hearts. With them God preserves the earth, and with them He destroys it if they are otherwise."

A., 64.—The Messiah (Peace be upon Him!) said, "Verily you will obtain what you like only by your patience with what you dislike."

A., 65.—I saw in the Gospel that Jesus, son of Mary (Peace be upon him!) said, "It has been said to you formerly, Tooth for tooth and nose for nose; but I say to you, Do not resist evil with evil. On the contrary, if someone strikes your right cheek, turn to him the left cheek; and if one takes your cloak give him your mantle;

and if one compels you to go a mile with him go with him two miles."

A., 68; *M.*, 60.—It is related concerning the Messiah (Blessing and peace be upon him!) that he said, "O company of the disciples, you fear acts of disobedience, but we, the companies of the prophets, fear infidelity."

A., 76; *M.*, 64.—It is related on the authority of our prophet [i.e. Mohammad] and on the authority of Jesus (Peace be upon them!), "Four things are attained only with trouble—silence, which is the beginning of worship; humility; much glorifying of God; and small possessions." [Cf. *A.*, 135, p. 55.]

A., 83.—Jesus (Peace be upon him!) said, "He is not wise who cannot rejoice at entering calamities and illnesses in his body and his wealth on account of what he hopes for from that of remission of his sins."

A., 85.—In the stories of Jesus (Peace be upon him!) [we read], "When you see a young man smitten with the search after God (Exalted is He!), then that has engrossed him to the neglect of everything else."

A., 87.—It is handed down in the Gospel, "When you give alms, do it so that your left hand does not know what your right hand has done; then he who sees the hidden things will reward you openly. And when you fast, wash your face and anoint your head, that no one other than your Lord may know of it." [Cf. A., 55, p. 46.]

A., 89; M., 68.—It is related that Jesus (Peace be upon him!) said to the Children of Israel, "Where does the seed grow?" They replied, "In the earth." Then he said, "Verily I say unto you, wisdom grows only in a heart like the earth."

A., 91; M., 70.—Jesus (Peace be upon him!) was asked about the best work, and he said, "Resignation to God (Exalted is He!) and love for Him."

A., 92; M., 71.—Jesus (Peace be upon him!) said, "Blessed is the eye which sleeps and does not think of disobedience, and awakes to sinlessness."

A., 94; M., 72.—The disciples said to Jesus, (Peace be upon him!) "What is the purest of deeds?" Then he replied, "[That of] him who works for God (Exalted is He!) not wishing anyone to praise him for it."

A., 96; M., 73.—Jesus (Peace be upon him!) said, "Things are of three kinds—one whose righteousness is clear, so follow it; another whose error is clear, so avoid it; and another which is doubtful to you, so commit it to him who knows it." [i.e. for him to give advice regarding it.]

A., 97; M., 74.—The disciples said to Jesus, son of Mary, "O Spirit of God, is there anyone in the earth like you to-day?" He replied,

Christ in Islam

"Yes; he whose talk is glorifying God, whose silence is meditation, and whose look is a tear; he is like me."

A., 100.—Jesus (Peace be upon him!) said, "Do not worry about to-morrow's food, for if to-morrow is one of your periods your provisions will come in it along with your periods; and if it is not one of your periods, do not worry about other people's periods."

A., 104.—They saw him coming out of a prostitute's house, then someone said to him, "O Spirit of God, what are you doing with this woman?" He replied, "The doctor comes only to the sick."

A., 105.—Jesus, son of Mary (The blessings of God—exalted is He!—be upon him!) said, "O company of the disciples, verily man is created in the world in four ranks, in three of which he is secure, but in the fourth of which he has evil thoughts, fearing that God will abandon him. As regards the first rank, he is created in three darknesses, the darkness of the belly, the darkness of the womb, and the darkness of the placenta; then God gives him his provision in the depth of the darkness of the belly. Then when he is taken out of the darkness of the belly, he comes to the milk. He does not step to it with foot or leg, or reach out to it with a hand, or leap to it with force; on the contrary, he is forced to it against his inclination and is guarded until his flesh and blood grow upon him. Then when he gets beyond milk, he comes into the third rank with respect to food from his parents which they acquire for him of what is allowable and what is forbidden. Then if they die, people are kindly-disposed to him. One gives him food, another gives him drink, another shelters him, and another clothes him. Then when he comes into the fourth rank and grows up and becomes a man, he fears that he will not be given provision, so he attacks men and betrays their trust and steals their goods and takes their possessions by force out of fear that God (Exalted is He!) may abandon him."

A., 107.—We are told concerning the Messiah (God bless him and grant him peace!) that he said, "If God shows generosity to one of His worshippers, His generosity is necessary for all His creatures."

A., 109.—In a tradition [it is said] that Jesus, son of Mary (Peace be upon him!) met a man and said to him, "What are you doing?" He replied, "I am devoting myself to God." He said, "Who is giving you what you need?" He said, "My brother." [Jesus] said, "He is more devoted to God than you."

A., 112.—Jesus (Peace be upon him!) said to the disciples, "Do not consider men's works as though you were lords, but consider your own works as though you were servants; for people are only of two kinds, tried and preserved. So have pity on those who are tried, and praise God for health."

A., 116.—And among the things which God sent down to the Messiah in the Gospel [we read], "We have made you desire, but you have not desired; and we have wailed to you, but you did not weep. O you of fifty years, what have you sent before and what have you left behind! O you of sixty years, your harvest has come near. O you of seventy years, come to the account."

A., 119.—The Messiah (God bless him and grant him peace!) passed by some people of the Children of Israel who were weeping, and said to them, "What makes you weep?" They replied, "We are weeping for our sins." He said, "Leave them alone; they are forgiven you."

A., 122.—We have been told about Jesus (Peace be upon him!) that someone said to him, "Who is the mightiest of men in seduction?" He replied, "The slip of a learned man; when he slips a world slips with him." [This saying contains a pun which cannot be reproduced in English. The word for "learned man" is *'ālim*, and for "world," *'ālam*.]

A., 127.—The Messiah (Peace be upon him!) passed some dyers outside the city and stopped beside them and said to them, "Do you think that when you have washed and purified and whitened these clothes, their owners will be right

Christ in Islam

in putting them on while their bodies are soiled with blood and urine and excrement and various kinds of filthiness?" They replied, "No, the one who did that would be foolish." He said, "You yourselves have done it." They said, "How?" He said, "Because you have purified your bodies and whitened your clothes while your souls are soiled with rottenness, full of filthiness from ignorance and blindness and dumbness and evil manners and envy and hatred and guile and deceit and covetousness and niggardliness and wickedness and evil thoughts and the pursuit of evil desires, and you are in the abasement of slavery, wretches for whom there is no rest but death and the grave." Then they said, "How shall we act? Is there any escape from seeking a livelihood?" He said, "Can you take pleasure in the kingdom of heaven where there is no death, or decrepitude, or pain, or illness, or hunger, or thirst, or fear, or grief, or poverty, or need, or weariness, or affliction, or care, or envy among its people, or hatred, or boasting, or pride? But on the contrary, brethren sit opposite one another on couches, glad and rejoicing in pleasure and bounty and favour and satisfaction and splendour and agreeableness, walking in the vastness of the spheres in the wideness of the heavens, and seeing the kingdom of the Lord of the worlds and beholding the angels round His throne, pure, celebrating the praise of their Lord with melodies and tunes the like of which men and jinn have never heard. And you will be with them for ever, not ageing, or dying, or hungering, or thirsting, or becoming ill, or fearing, or grieving."

A., 130.—Jesus, son of Mary (Peace be upon him!), in what Ibn al Hamal the Christian scribe told us, said to his disciples, "The sign by which you are known as being from me is that you love one another." And Jesus said also to Joshua, his disciple, "As regards the Lord, you must love him with all your heart, then love your neighbour as you love yourself." They said to him, "Explain to us, O Spirit of God, what is the difference between these two loves, so that we may prepare for them with discernment and clearness." He said, "You love your friend for yourself, and you love yourself for your Lord; so when you guard your friend you do it for yourself, and when you are bountiful yourself you are so towards your Lord."

A., 132.—Jesus, son of Mary (God's blessings be upon him!), said to the disciples, "O salt of the earth, do not become bad, for when things become bad they can be treated only with salt, but when salt becomes bad it cannot be treated with anything. O company of the disciples, do not take remuneration from those whom you teach, except like what you have given me. And know that there are two characteristics of ignorance in you—laughter without anything extraordinary, and sleeping in the morning without a [previous] vigil."

A., 134.—Jesus said to the Children of Israel, "Do not reward an evil-doer with evil, for your favour will go for nothing with your Lord."

A., 135.—This word is handed down from Jesus, son of Mary (Peace be upon him!), "Four things are found only in a believer: silence which is the beginning of devotion, humility, glorifying of God (Exalted is He!), and a small amount of evil." [Cf. A., 76; M., 64, p. 48.]

A., 136.—It is related concerning Jesus, son of Mary (Peace be upon him!), that he said, "Every word which is not accompanied by mention of God is vanity; and every silence which is not accompanied by meditation is negligence; and every speculation which is not accompanied by a tear is folly. So blessed is he whose speech is mention of God, whose silence is meditation, and whose speculation is a tear."

A., 140.—It is written in the Gospel, "He who sows evil reaps remorse."

A., 141.—It is related concerning Katāda that he said: It was mentioned to us that [the following] is written in the Gospel, "O son of man, as you show pity so will you be pitied; for how can you hope that God will pity you if you do not show pity to His servants?"

Christ in Islam

A., 142.—Mālik, son of Anas (God—Exalted is He!—be pleased with him!), said: It has reached me that Jesus (God's blessings and peace be upon him!) said, "Do not speak much without mention of God, or your hearts will become hard, and the hard heart is far from God (Exalted is He!); but you do not know."

A., 144.—[The following] is quoted from Jesus, son of Mary (Peace be upon them!), "What is the use of a blind man carrying a lamp while others get light from it? And what is the use of a dark house having a lamp on its roof? And what is the use of your speaking with wisdom and not acting with it?"

A., 150.—It is related concerning Jesus, son of Mary (Blessing and peace be upon him!), that he said, "There is nothing wonderful about one perishing in the way he perishes, but there is something wonderful about one being saved in the way he is saved."

A., 153.—Jesus said, "If Thou punishest them they are Thy servants, and if Thou forgivest them Thou art the mighty and the wise One." [Korān V, 118.]

A., 154.—In the Gospel [there is written], "I am the prince of life and the ways of truth; whoever believes in me and dies, has not died a death but has only lived a life." [Cf. John xiv. 6, xi. 25, 26.]

Christ in Islam

A., 155.—Jesus (Peace be upon him!) said to the disciples, "Verily I say unto you, the speaker of wisdom and the hearer of it are partners, and the one of them who is more worthy of it is he who verifies it by his deeds."

A., 156.—It is related that Jesus (Peace be upon him!) said to the disciples, "I do not teach you that you should wonder; I only teach you that you should act. Wisdom is not talking wisely; wisdom is only acting wisely."

A., 157.—Jesus said, "If you are able to be simple like a dove concerning God, then do so; nothing is more simple than a dove. You may take its two young from under it and kill them, and it will return to that very place and bring forth [others] in it."

A., 158.—Jesus said, "Speak much to God and speak little to men." They said, "How shall we speak much to God?" He said, "Be apart in intercourse with Him; be apart in prayer to Him."

A., 163.—Jesus, son of Mary (Peace be upon him!), said, "The steps slip only with regard to three things: smallness of thanks for God's gifts (Exalted is He!), fear of something other than God, and hope in created things."

A., 166.—Jesus (Peace be upon him!) said, "I am not incapable of raising the dead, but I am incapable of applying a remedy to the fool." [Cf. M., 5.]

A., 167; M., 32.—Jesus (Peace be upon him!)

said, "Verily one of the greatest sins in God's eyes is that a servant [of His] should say 'God knows,' when he is ignorant."

A., 173.—Jesus, son of Mary (Peace be upon him!), said, "The world consists of three days:—yesterday which has passed, from which you have nothing in your hand; to-morrow of which you do not know whether you will reach it or not; and to-day in which you are, so avail yourself of it."

A., 175.—Jesus (Peace be upon him!) said, "The recollection of the eternity of those who live for ever rends the hearts of those who fear God." [Asin interprets "those who live for ever" as "the damned," which gives good sense; but the literal translation is as above, with no reference to a particular class.]

A., 176.—The Messiah (Peace be upon him!) said, "O company of the disciples, how many lamps has the wind put out, and how many worshippers has self-conceit spoiled!"

A., 177.—Jesus said to John [the Baptist] (Peace be upon them!), "When a man admonishes you about something and says concerning you what is true, thank God (Great is His glory!); and if it is false, increase your thanks, for it flourishes in the register of your good deeds and you are at rest."

A., 180.—Jesus (Peace be upon him!) said, "God sent this revelation to the world, Whoever serves Me, serve him, and whoever serves you, take him as your servant."

A., 184.—Al Bokhārī related on the authority of Abū Huraira that the prophet—i.e. Mohammad—(God bless him and grant him peace!) said: Jesus, son of Mary, saw a man stealing and said to him, "Are you stealing?" He replied, "By no means! [I swear] by Him than whom there is no God!" Then Jesus (Peace be upon him!) said, "You believe in God, and you have accused my eye of falsehood!"

A., 185.—The Messiah (Peace be upon him!) said, "What is the forbearance of him who has not been patient with foolishness, and what is the strength of him who has not repelled anger, and what is the worship of him who has not been humble towards his Lord? (Exalted is He!) The worship of the foolish is the coming at the wrong time and the sitting beyond what is decreed; but when necessity arises counsel disappears."

A., 188.—Jesus (Peace be upon him!) said, "If you bear with one word from a foolish man you will profit tenfold."

A., 190.—There has been handed down from Jesus (God's blessings be upon him!), "He who has not been born twice shall not enter the kingdom of heaven." [Cf. *A.*, 207, p. 61.]

A., 191.—It is related concerning Jesus (Peace be upon him!) that he said, "Verily God (Exalted is He!) hates him who laughs immoderately without reason, and him who walks about without an aim, and talk which comes between jesting and facetiousness."

A., 192.—The upright Jesus (Peace be upon him!) has said, "Every man's heart is where his wealth is; so place your wealth in heaven that your hearts may be in heaven."

A., 194.—Jesus (Blessing and peace be upon him!) gave the following injunction to one of his companions, "Fast from the world, and do not cease from your fast till you die, and be like him who treats his sore with medicine out of fear that it may become worse to him. And occupy yourself much with the thought of death; for death brings good to the believer with no evil after it, but evil to the wicked with no good after it."

A., 196.—From the book of Interpretations [or, Biographies] [we are told] that Jesus (Peace be upon him!) said, "Associate with people in such a way that if you live they may long for you, and if you die they may weep for you."

A., 200.—A man asked Jesus (Peace be upon him!) "Who is the best of men?" Then he took two handfuls of earth and said, "Which of these two is the better? Men were created from earth, so the most honourable of them is the most God-fearing of them."

A., 204.—It is related on the authority of Ibrāhīm, son of Adham, that Jesus (Peace be upon him!) said, "The honour of a believer with God is that he should say to a mountain, 'Move,' then it should move."

A., 205.—It is related on the authority of Ma'rūf al Karkhī that Jesus (Peace be upon him!) said, "Remember cotton when it is put over your eyes."

A., 207.—A saying of Jesus, son of Mary, "O, Children of Israel, verily I say unto you, he who has not been born twice will not see the kingdom of the heavens and the earth. By God, verily we are of those who have been born twice. The first birth is the birth of nature, and the second birth is the birth of the spirit in the heaven of knowledge." [Cf. A., 190, p. 59.]

A., 209.—Sufyān al Thaurī used to say: "A man said to Jesus, son of Mary (Blessing and peace be upon him!), "Give me some advice." He replied, "Consider where your bread comes from."

A., 217.—It is related on the authority of Sālim, son of Abu al Ja'd, that Jesus (Peace be upon him!) said, "Blessed is he who weeps for his sin, and who stores away his tongue, and whose house contains him."

A., 225.—There is handed down from Jesus (Peace be upon him!), "The wise are of three kinds: he who knows God and God's command, he who knows God and does not know God's command, and he who knows God's command and does not know God."

Christ in Islam

[The following passages are not included in Asin's collection. I give Professor Margoliouth's rendering of them along with his note on one of them.]

M., 2.—Jesus said: The world is a place of transition, full of examples; be pilgrims therein, and take warning by the traces of those that have gone before.

M., 3.—Jesus said: Be in the midst, yet walk on one side. [This is variously interpreted. Some say it means, Be in the world, yet let thy heart be in heaven; the context, however, in which it is quoted deals with cases in which it is necessary to avow friendship while concealing enmity.]

M., 4.—In the sermons of Jesus, son of Mary, it is written: Beware how you sit with sinners.

M., 6.—God revealed unto Jesus: Command the children of Israel that they enter not my house save with pure hearts, and humble eyes, and clean hands; for I will not answer any one of them against whom any has a complaint.

M., 13.—Jesus said: If a man send away a beggar empty from his house, the angels will not visit that house for seven nights.

M., 19.—When Jesus was asked, How art thou this morning? he would answer, Unable to forestall what I hope, or to put off what I fear, bound by my works, with all my good in another's hand. There is no poor man poorer than I.

Chapter 4
Ascetic Sayings

A., 6; *M.*, 11.—Jesus (Peace be upon him!) said, "How can he be one of the learned whose journey is towards the next world and who is turning towards the way of the present world? And how can he be one of the learned who seeks words to report them, and not to act according to them?"

A., 20; *M.*, 24.—Jesus (Peace be upon him!) said, "Blessed is he who abandons a present desire for a distant promise which he has not seen."

A., 21; *M.*, 25.—Jesus (Peace be upon him!) said, "Make your livers hungry and your bodies naked; perhaps your hearts may see God (Great and glorious is He!)"

A., 22; *M.*, 26.—It is related that Jesus (Peace be upon him!) remained for sixty days in secret communion with his Lord without eating. Then the thought of bread occurred to him, and the communion ceased, and behold a loaf was placed before him. Then he sat down weeping over the loss of the communion. Then behold an old man approached him, and Jesus said to him,

Christ in Islam

"God bless you, O friend of God! Pray for me to God (Exalted is He!), for I was in an ecstasy and the thought of bread occurred to me, and the ecstasy ceased." Then the old man said, "O God, if Thou knowest that the thought of bread has occurred to me since I have known Thee, then do not pardon me. On the contrary, whenever anything came to me, I ate it without thought or consideration."

A., 26; M., 29.—Jesus (Peace be upon him!) said, "Devotion has ten parts, nine of which are found in silence and one in flight from men."

A., 30.—John [the Baptist] said to Jesus (Peace be upon them!), "Do not be angry." He replied, "I am unable to keep from anger; I am only a man." He said, "Do not acquire wealth." He replied, "This is possible."

A., 34; M., 35.—Jesus (Peace be upon him!) said, "Do not take the world as a master, for it will take you as slaves. Lay up your treasure with him who will not lose it, for he who possesses treasure in this world fears lest some calamity may come upon it, but he who possesses God's treasure has no fear of calamity coming upon it."

A., 34; M., 36.—And he said (The richest blessing and peace be upon him!), "O company of the disciples, I have overturned the world for you on its face, so do not raise it up after me. For part of the wickedness of the world is that disobedience to God is in it; and part of the wickedness of the world is that the next world is attained only by abandoning it. Is it not so? Therefore pass through the world, but do not stay in it; and know that the root of all sin is the love of the world. And the desire of an hour often leaves those who indulge in it an inheritance of grief which lasts for long."

A., 34; *M.*, 37.—And he said also, "I have thrown down the world for you and you have sat on its back, so let not kings or women quarrel with you about it. As regards kings, do not quarrel with them about the world, for they will not oppose you so long as you leave them and their world alone; and as regards women, protect yourselves against them by fasting and prayer."

A., 34; *M.*, 38.—And he said also, "The world is both seeking and sought. He who seeks the next world, this world seeks him until his provision in it is complete; and he who seeks the present world, the next world seeks him until death comes and seizes him by the neck."

A., 35; *M.*, 39.—Jesus (Peace be upon him!) said, "The love of this world and of the next cannot stay in the heart of a believer, just as water and fire cannot stay in one vessel."

A., 36; *M.*, 40.—Someone said to Jesus (Peace be upon him!), "If you were to take a house to cover you [it would be good]." He replied, "The rags of those who lived before us are sufficient for us."

Christ in Islam

A., 37; *M.*, 41.—It is related that one day the rain and thunder and lightning were fierce about Jesus (Peace be upon him!), so he began to seek something under which he might shelter. His eye fell on a tent far off, so he came to it; but behold there was a woman in it, so he turned away from it. Then he saw a cave in a hill and came to it, but behold there was a lion in it. Then he put his hand on it and said, "My God, Thou hast given everything an abode, and Thou hast not given me an abode." Then God (Exalted is He!) revealed to him, "Your abode is in the dwelling of My mercy. Verily I will give to you in marriage on the Day of Resurrection a hundred houris whom I have created with My hand, and I will give a feast at your wedding for four thousand years, each day of which is like the duration of the present world, and I will command one to proclaim, 'Where are those who were ascetics in the world? Visit the marriage of the ascetic in the world, Jesus, son of Mary.'"

A., 38; *M.*, 42.—Jesus, son of Mary (Peace be upon him!) said, "Woe to him who loves the world! How can he die and leave it and what is in it! It deceives him, yet he trusts in it and puts his confidence in it and he is taken away. And woe to those who are deceived! How what they abhor has caused dissension among them, and what they like has left them, and what they p. 67were threatened with has come to them! And woe to him whose care is the world, and whose work is sins! How he shall be covered with shame to-morrow for his offence!"

A., 40; *M.*, 43.—Jesus (Peace be upon him!) said, "Who is he who builds a house on the wave of the sea? The world is [like] that, so do not take it as an abiding place."

A., 41; *M.*, 44.—Some people said to Jesus (Peace be upon him!), "Teach us one piece of knowledge for which God will love us." He replied, "Hate the world, and God (Exalted is He!) will love you."

A., 42; *M.*, 45.—Jesus (Peace be upon him!) said, "O company of the disciples, be pleased with what is worthless in the world along with welfare in religion, just as the people of the world are pleased with what is worthless in religion along with welfare in the world."

A., 43; *M.*, 46.—The Messiah (Peace be upon him!) said, "O you who seek the world to be charitable with it, your leaving of it alone is more charitable." And he said, "The least thing is such that looking after it occupies one to the exclusion of glorifying God, and glorifying God is greater and more important."

A., 44; *M.*, 47.—If you wish you may follow him who was the Spirit and the Word, Jesus, son of Mary (Peace be upon him!), for he used to say, "My seasoning is hunger, my under-garment is fear [of God], my outer-garment is wool, my fire in winter is the rays of the sun, my lamp is the moon, my riding-beast is my feet, and my food and fruit are what the earth brings forth [i.e. without cultivation]. At night I have nothing and in the morning I have nothing, yet there is no one on earth richer than I."

A., 45; *M.*, 48.—It is related that the world was revealed to Jesus (Peace be upon him!) and he saw it in the form of a toothless old woman upon whom was every kind of ornament. Then he said to her, "How many have you married?" She replied, "I cannot count them." He said, "Did they all die and leave you, or did they all divorce you?" She said, "Nay, I killed them all." Then Jesus (Peace be upon him!) said, "It is a pity for the rest of your husbands. How do they not take warning from your past husbands how you have been destroying them one after another, and [how] are they not on their guard against you! "

A., 46.—Jesus (Peace be upon him!) said, "The world is a bridge, so pass over it and do not inhabit it." [Cf. *A.*, 75, p. 71.]

A., 47; *M.*, 49.—Jesus (Peace be upon him!) said, "Verily I say unto you, as a sick man looks at food and takes no delight in it because of the severity of the pain, so he who loves the world takes no delight in worship and does not discover its sweetness along with what he finds of love of the world. And verily I say unto you, if a riding-beast is not ridden and taken into service, it becomes intractable and its nature changes; similarly when hearts are not softened by the thought of death and the discipline of worship, they become hard and coarse. And verily I say unto you, as long as a skin is not torn or shrivelled it may nearly serve as a receptacle for honey; similarly hearts, as long as desires do not tear them, or greed defile them, or comfort harden them, may be vessels for wisdom."

A., 48; *M.*, 50.—Jesus (Peace be upon him!) said, "He who seeks after the world is like one who drinks sea-water; the more he drinks the more his thirst increases, until it kills him."

A., 49; *M.*, 51.—The disciples said to Jesus (Peace be upon him!), "How is it that you can walk on water and we cannot?" Then he said to them, "What do you think of the dīnār and the dirhem?" [*pieces of money*]. They replied, "They are good." He said, "But they and mud are alike to me." [Cf. *A.*, 126, p. 74.]

A., 50; *M.*, 52.—Jesus (Blessing and peace be upon him!) said, "In wealth there are calamities: that one should get it unlawfully." Someone interrupted, "Suppose one gets it lawfully?" Then he said, "He may apply it unlawfully." The other said, "But suppose he applies it lawfully?" Then he said, "Its management occupies him to the neglect of God (Exalted is He!)."

A., 60; *M.*, 57.—Jesus (Peace be upon him!) said, "Fine clothing is vanity of heart."

A., 63 (Cf. *M.*, 22).—Jesus (Peace be upon him!) attained to the use of a stone for his pillow while sleeping; but the devil came to him and said, "Have you not renounced this world for the next?" He said, "Yes, but what has happened?" Then he said, "Your use of this stone as a pillow means that you are being comfortable in the world; so why do you not put your head on the ground?" Then Jesus (Peace be upon him!) threw away the stone and put his head on the ground.

A., 70; *M.*, 61.—The Messiah (Peace be upon him!) said, "O companies of the disciples, fear of God and love of Paradise produce patience in affliction and estrange men from the world. Verily I say unto you, eating barley and sleeping on dunghills with dogs is a small matter when one seeks Paradise."

A., 71; *M.*, 62.—It is related that the Messiah (God bless him and grant him peace!) passed in his wandering a man asleep wrapped up in his cloak; then he wakened him and said, "O sleeper, arise and glorify God (Exalted is He!)." Then the man said, "What do you want from me? Verily I have abandoned the world to its people." So he said to him, "Sleep, then, my friend."

Christ in Islam

A., 72.—The Messiah (God bless him and grant him peace!) said, "With difficulty does a rich man enter heaven."

A., 73; M., 18.—The Messiah (God's blessings and peace be upon him!) said, "Verily I love poverty and hate comfort." And the dearest of names to him (God's blessings be upon him!) was that he should be called, "O poor one."

A., 74; M., 63.—The Messiah (Peace be upon him!) said, "Do not look at the wealth of the people of this world, for the splendour of their wealth takes away the light of your faith."

A., 75.—The Messiah (God bless him and grant him peace!) said, "The world is a bridge, so pass over it and do not inhabit it." And some people said to him, "O prophet of God, if you would only order us to build a house in which we might worship God!" He replied, "Go and build a house on water." They said, "How will a building stand on water?" He replied, "And how will worship stand along with love of this world?" [Cf. A., 46, p. 68.]

A., 77.—'Obaid, son of 'Omair, said, The Messiah, son of Mary (Peace be upon him!) used to wear hair clothing, and eat wild fruits [lit. trees], and he had no son to die, and no house to be demolished, and he stored up nothing for the morrow. He slept wherever the evening overtook him. [Cf. A., 118, p. 73.]

Christ in Islam

A., 79.—Jesus (Peace be upon him!) sat down in the shade of someone's wall, and the owner of the wall made him get up. Then he said, "You have not made me get up; He who has made me get up is only He [i.e. God] who was not pleased that I should be comfortable in the shade of the wall."

A., 80.—The Messiah (God bless him and grant him peace!) used to say, "O Children of Israel, use pure water and wild vegetables and barley bread, and avoid wheaten bread, for you will not remain thankful to God."

A., 81; *M.*, 65.—Jesus, the Messiah (God's blessings and peace be upon him!), used to take nothing with him but a comb and a jug. Then he saw a man combing his beard with his fingers, so he threw away the comb; and he saw another drinking from a river with the palms of his hands, so he threw away the jug.

A., 82.—Jesus (Peace be upon him!) said, "Look at the birds; they do not sow, or harvest, or store up, yet God (Exalted is He!) feeds them day by day. But if you say, We have larger bellies, look at the cattle, how God (Exalted is He!) has appointed for them this creation as provision."

A., 146.—Mohammad, son of al Fadl, told us on the authority of Sālim, son of Abū al Ja'd (God be pleased with him!) that Jesus, son of Mary (God's blessings and peace be upon him!), said, "Do not store food for the morrow, for the morrow comes bringing along with it its provision. And look at the ants and who gives them provision. But if you say, The ants' bellies are small, look at the bird. And if you say, The bird has wings, look at the wild beasts, how corpulent and fat they are."

A., 86; *M.*, 66.—Someone said to Jesus (Peace be upon him!), "Why do you not buy an ass to ride?" Then he replied, "I am too dear to God (Exalted is He!) for Him to allow me to be occupied with an ass to the neglect of Himself."

A., 103.—Jesus (Peace be upon him!) said, "How many healthy bodies and beautiful faces and eloquent tongues will lie to-morrow among the strata of hell!"

A., 111.—Jesus (Peace be upon him!) said to the disciples, "Take the mosques as houses and the houses as alighting-places; and eat wild vegetables and drink pure water, and escape safe from the world."

A., 113.—Jesus (Peace be upon him!) said to the disciples, "It is astonishing how you work for this world, yet you receive provision in it without work; and how you do not work for the next world, yet you receive provision in it only with work."

A., 117.—The Messiah (Peace be upon him!) said, "The world is a field belonging to Iblīs [Satan], and its people are his ploughmen."

A., 118.—The Messiah (Blessing and peace be upon him!) said to the disciples, "I am he who has inverted the world on its face; so I have no wife to die and no house to be demolished." [Cf. *A.*, 77, p. 71.]

A., 123.—Jesus (Peace be upon him!) used to say to the world, "Away from me, O swine!"

A., 125.—Jesus (Peace be upon him!) used to say, "The sweetness of this world is the bitterness of the next, and fine clothes are vanity of heart, meaning conceit and pride of heart; and fullness of the belly is abundance of passion, meaning its sustenance and its accumulation." [Cf. *A.*, 60; *M.*, 57, p. 70.]

A., 126.—The disciples said, "O Spirit of God, we pray as you pray, and we fast as you fast, and we glorify God (Exalted is He!) as you have ordered us, yet we are unable to walk on the water as you do." Then he said, "Tell me how your love of the world is." They replied, "Verily we love it." So he said, "Verily the love of it spoils religion, but in my opinion it is merely like stone and mud." And in another story [it is said] that he lifted up a stone and asked, "Which of the two is dearer to you, this or a dīnār and a dirhem?" They replied, "A dīnār." He said, "They are both alike to me." [Cf. *A.*, 49; *M.*, 51, p. 69.]

A., 139.—If you desire the fast of the son of the virgin maid, meaning Jesus, son of Mary (Peace be upon them!), then he used to fast all the time and eat barley bread and wear

Christ in Islam

coarse hair; and wherever the night overtook him he used to arrange his feet in prayer until he saw that the sign of the dawn had arisen; and he never stayed anywhere without praying two rek'as in it. And if you desire the fast of his mother, then she used to fast for two days and break her fast for two days.

A., 145.—It is mentioned concerning Jesus, son of Mary (Blessing and peace be upon him!), that he went out one day to his companions wearing a woollen tunic, a woollen outer-garment, and clothes of wool, with his head and his moustaches shorn, weeping and looking pale from hunger, with his lips dry from thirst, with the hair on his chest and arms long; then he said, "Peace be upon you! Verily I am he who has lowered the world in its rank by the permission of God, and there is no wonder or boasting. O Children of Israel, despise the world and it will be easy for you, and scorn the world and the next world will be made honourable for you, and do not despise the next world and this world will be made honourable for you. For the world is not worthy of honour; every day it calls to temptation and loss." Then he said, "If you are my companions and friends, accustom yourselves to enmity and hatred towards the world, for if you do not do so, you are not my friends or my brethren. O Children of Israel, take the mosques as houses, and the graves as homes;

be like guests. Do you not see the birds of the heaven? they do not sow or reap, and God in heaven gives them provision. O Children of Israel, eat barley bread and wild vegetables; and know that you have not given thanks for that, so how about what is more than that?"

A., 162.—Jesus (Peace be upon him!) said, "This world in relation to the next is like a man who has two wives; if he is pleased with one of them, he is displeased with the other."

A., 168.—It is related that Jesus (Peace be upon him!) passed by a man asleep on the ground with a brick under his head and his face and his beard in the dust, and he had a woollen cloak tied round him. Then he said, "O Lord, this servant of Thine is astray in the world." Then God (Exalted is He!) revealed to him, "O Jesus, do you not know that when I look at My servant with my whole face, I remove from him the whole world?"

A., 169.—Jesus (Peace be upon him!) said, "Verily I have two friends; he who loves them loves me, and he who hates them hates me:—poverty and distress."

A., 174 bis.—In the Israelite history it is said that Iblīs [Satan] appeared to Jesus (Peace be upon him!), and he saw things hanging on him coloured with all kinds of dyes. Then he said to him, "What are these hanging things?" He replied, "These are the desires of the children of men."

Christ in Islam

Then he asked, "Is there anything of mine among them?" He replied, "You have often eaten your fill and we have made you too heavy for prayer and for glorifying God." He asked, "Is there anything else?" He replied, "No." He said, "I swear to God that I will never fill my belly with food." Iblīs said, "And I swear to God that I will never advise a Muslim."

A., 193.—Jesus (Blessing and peace be upon him!) said, "O Children of Israel, know that the relation of your present life to your future life is like the relation of the east to the west. The more you approach the east, the farther you are from the west; and the more you approach the west, the farther do you increase in distance from the east."

A., 220.—Jesus (Peace be upon him!) struck the ground with his hand and took up some of it and spread it out, and behold, he had gold in one of his hands and clay in the other. Then he said to his companions, "Which of them is sweeter to your hearts?" They said, "The gold." He said, "They are both alike to me." [Cf. A., 49; M., 51, p. 69; and A., 126, p. 74.]

A., 221.—Jesus, son of Mary (Peace be upon him!), said, "By God, the world has not settled in the heart of a worshipper without three of its things sticking to it: labour whose distress does not cease, poverty which does not catch up on its wealth, and hope which does not attain its goal."

Chapter 5
Sayings of God to Jesus

A., 7; M., 12.—God (Exalted is He!) said to Jesus (Peace be upon him!), "O son of Mary, exhort yourself, then if you take warning, exhort men; otherwise be ashamed before Me."

A., 14; M., 15.—It is related that God (Exalted is He!) sent this revelation to Jesus (Peace be upon him!), "Though you should worship Me like the people of the heavens and the earth and had not love in God and hate in God, it would avail you nothing."

A., 58.—It is said that God (Exalted is He!) revealed to Jesus (Peace be upon him!), "When I bestow a favour on you, receive it with humility and I will make it perfect for you."

A., 90; M., 69.—God revealed to Jesus (Peace be upon him!), "When I consider the secret thoughts of a worshipper and do not find in him love of this world or of the next, I fill him with love of Me and take him under My care."

A., 124.—We are told concerning Jesus (Peace be upon him!) among the things that God

Christ in Islam

(Exalted is He!) revealed to him [the following], "O son of man, weep during the days of your life like him who takes leave of the world and whose desire is raised to the things which are with God (Exalted is He!). Be satisfied with mere subsistence from the world. Let what is coarse and rough satisfy you from it. Verily I say unto you, you remain only your day and your hour. What you have received from the world and that on which you have spent it are written concerning you. So work in accordance with this, for you are responsible for it. If you were to see what I have promised the upright, your soul would pass away."

A., 133.—And it is said that there is written in the Gospel, "O son of man, remember Me when you are angry and I shall remember you when I am angry; and be pleased with My help to you, for My help to you is better than your help to yourself."

A., 223.—God (Praise be to Him!) said to Jesus, "Verily the world is not good except with wheat and barley; so their going bad is not good, for they are the dearest parts of My creation to Me. O Jesus, know that the seed has an honour which no creature's honour resembles, and I am angry with him who spoils it just as I am angry with him who says that I am the third of three [with reference to the doctrine of the Trinity], or as I am angry with him who says that I am poor, or as I am angry with him who declares that I have begotten a son, until he renounces what he has done and repents of the evil he has committed. Then I forgive him, for I am the Forgiver of offences."

Chapter 6
Miscellaneous Passages

A., 11; *M.*, 14.—The prayer of Jesus (God bless him and grant him peace!). He used to say, "O God, I am unable to drive away what I dislike, and to get the benefit of what I hope for. The affair is in the hands of another, and I am put under obligation by my work, and there is no poor one who is poorer than I. O God, do not let my enemy exult over me, or my friend be offended with me; and do not make my misfortune to be with respect to my religion; and do not make the world my greatest care; and do not let him who will not pity me have power over me, O Living One, O Everlasting One."

A., 17; *M.*, 20.—It is related that Satan (God curse him!) appeared to Jesus, son of Mary (God bless him and grant him peace!) and said to him, "Say, There is no God but God." Then he replied, "It is a word of truth, but I will not say it at your request, for beneath what is good it has also ambiguities."

A., 18; *M.*, 21.—It is related that when Jesus, son of Mary (Peace be upon him!) was born, the devils came to Iblīs [Satan] and said, "This morning the idols have been thrown down on their heads." Then he said, "This is a new thing which has happened. Remain where you are." Then he flew till he came to the East and the West of the earth, but found nothing. Afterwards he found Jesus (Peace be upon him!) already born with the angels doing him honour. Then he returned to them and said, "Verily a prophet has been born last night; no woman ever became pregnant or gave birth to a child without my being present, with the exception of this [child]. So despair of the idols being worshipped after this night; but attack the sons of men from the side of haste and levity."

A., 53; *M.*, 54.—It has reached us that Jesus, son of Mary (Peace be upon him!) said, "O you learned men who are evil, you fast and pray and give alms, and do not do what you are commanded, and you teach what you do not perform. How evil is what you decide! You repent in speech and hopes, but act according to desire. What does it avail you to purify your skins while your hearts are filthy? Verily I say unto you, do not be like a sieve from which the good flour goes out and in which the siftings remain. Similarly you utter the decree from your mouths, while malice remains in your hearts. O slaves of the world, how can he attain the next world whose desire is not fulfilled in this world and whose craving is not cut off from it? Verily I say unto you, your hearts will weep for your deeds. You have put the world under your tongues and [good] deeds under your feet. Verily I say unto you, you have spoiled your next life, for the welfare of the present world is dearer to you than the welfare of the next. So what men are greater losers than you, if you only knew it! Woe to you! How long will you describe the way to those who journey by night and remain as people who are confused, as though you were calling the people of the world to leave it to you? Gently, gently! Woe to you! What does it avail a dark house if a lamp is placed on its roof when inside is black darkness? Similarly it will not avail you that the light of knowledge should be in your mouths when your inner parts are waste and uncultivated respecting it. O slaves of the world, you are not pious like slaves, or honourable like freemen. The world will soon uproot you and throw you on your faces, then it will overturn you on your nostrils; then your sons will seize your forelocks and thrust you from behind you, until they hand you over to the Royal Judge, naked and ruined. Then He will make you think of your baseness and will requite you for the evil of your deeds."

A., 61; *M.*, 58.—Jesus (Peace be upon him!) said, "Why do you come to me wearing monks' clothing while your hearts are the hearts of ravenous wolves? Put on king's clothing and mortify your hearts with fear."

A., 98; *M.*, 75.—When Jesus (Peace be upon him!) thought of death his skin used to drop blood.

A., 101; *M.*, 76.—Jesus (Peace be upon him!) said, "O company of the disciples, pray to God (Exalted is He!) that He may make easy for me this intoxication (meaning death), for I fear death in such a way that my fear of it has bequeathed it to me." [Probably meaning that the fear of death is as severe as the pains of death themselves.]

A., 108.—Jesus, son of Mary (Peace be upon him!) said, "In the last days there will be learned men who teach abstinence in the world but will not be abstinent themselves, who will teach men to take delight in the next world but will not take delight in it themselves, and who will warn men against coming before rulers but will not refrain themselves. They will draw near the rich and keep far away from the poor; they will be pleasant to great men but will shrink from humble men. Those are the brethren of the devils and the enemies of the Merciful."

A., 110.—Jesus, son of Mary (Peace be upon them!) said to the disciples, "Woe to you, slaves of the world! How do your branches differ from your roots and your desires from

Christ in Islam

your minds! Your speech is a remedy which could cure disease, but your action is a disease which is not amenable to treatment. Are you not like the vine whose leaves are beautiful, whose fruit is good, and whose growth is easy? But you are like the acacia whose leaves are few, whose thorns are many, and whose growth is difficult. Woe to you, slaves of the world! You have put action under your feet; whoever wishes may take it. And you have put the world over your heads; it cannot be taken. You are neither sincere slaves nor honourable freemen. Woe to you, whelps of evil! You take the reward but spoil the work. You will meet what you are on your guard against when the Lord of the work considers His work which you have spoiled and His reward which you have taken."

A., 115.—The Messiah (God bless him and grant him peace!) said, "The friends of God, upon whom there is no fear and who do not grieve [this phrase occurs frequently in the Korān. Cf. II, 36 etc.], are they who look into the inner things of the world when men look at its outward things, and at its hereafter when men look at its present. They have mortified what they feared would kill them, and have abandoned what they knew would abandon them. They are the enemies of what makes peace with men and make peace with what is hostile to men. For them is a wonderful good and with them is the

Christ in Islam

wonderful good. Of them the Scripture spoke and of it they speak. With them is the knowledge of right guidance and they are acquainted with it. They see no security apart from what they hope for, and no fear apart from what they are on their guard against."

A., 115a.—It has been related in the ancient books that the disciples said to Jesus (Peace be upon him!), "O Spirit of God, describe to us the friends of God (Exalted is He!) upon whom there is no fear, and who do not grieve." Then he (Peace be upon him!) said, "They," etc. . . . "their remembrance in it is death and their joy in it is grief [i.e. in the world]. Whatever of it encounters them they reject, and whatever of it is elevated to them they put down. The world is bad in their sight and they do not renew it; and it has gone to ruin among them and they do not build it; and it has died in their breasts and they do not bring it back to life after its death; and they have built their next life in it. They have brought to life the remembrance of death and they have mortified the remembrance of life. They love God and keep alive His remembrance, and they seek for themselves in Him the good and wonderful light," etc.

A., 128.—It was a custom of the Messiah's to go every day from village to village of the villages of Palestine and from town to town of the habitations of the Children of Israel, curing

Christ in Islam

people and preaching to them and admonishing them and summoning them to the kingdom of heaven and making them take pleasure in it and making them practise asceticism in the world and making clear to them its deceitfulness and its hopes. And he was sought by the king of the Children of Israel and by the rabble; and while he was among a company of people, so that a rush was made at him that he might be taken, he turned aside among the people and it was impossible to catch him, and nothing was known of him until news of him came from another village, so he was sought there; and that was his custom and their custom for thirty months [i.e. he kept eluding them for that period]. Then when God (Exalted is He!) wished to take him and raise him to Himself, his disciples gathered with him in Jerusalem in a room belonging to one [*fem.*] of his companions, and he said, "Verily I am going to my Father and your Father, and I am giving you an injunction before the departure of my divine nature and am making with you a covenant and a pledge. So he who receives my injunction and fulfils my covenant will be with me to-morrow; but he who does not receive my injunction, I have nothing to do with him, and he has nothing to do with me." Then they said to him, "What is it?" He replied, "Go to the kings of the ends of the earth and convey to them what I

Christ in Islam

have charged you with, and summon them to that to which I have summoned you, and do not deceive them, and do not fear them, for when I leave my humanity I shall be standing in heaven at the right hand of the throne of my Father and your Father, and shall be with you wherever you go and shall strengthen you with help and strength by the permission of my Father. Go to them and summon them with gentleness and cure them and command them to be kind and forbid them what is unlawful, until you are killed, or crucified, or rejected from the earth." Then they asked, "What is the verification of what you command us?" He replied, "I am the first who does that." And he went out the next day and appeared to the people and began to summon them and admonish them and warn them until he was taken and carried to the king of the Children of Israel. Then he ordered him to be crucified, and his humanity was crucified and his hands were nailed to the two pieces of wood of the cross, and he remained on the cross from dawn to afternoon. And he asked for water, and was given vinegar to drink, and he was pierced with a lance. Then he was buried where the cross was and forty people were put in charge of the grave; and all this happened in the presence of his companions and his disciples. Then when they saw that happen to him, they were sure and

Christ in Islam

knew that he had commanded them nothing in which he was different from them. Three days afterwards they gathered in the place where he promised them to appear to them and they saw those signs which [had been arranged] between him and them; and the news spread among the Children of Israel that the Messiah had not been killed. Then the grave was dug up, and the humanity was not found. The parties among them disagreed, and there was a great amount of talk which is too long to be recounted. Then verily those disciples who had accepted his injunction separated in the country and each of them went his own way. One went to the west, one to Abyssinia, two to Rome, two to the king of Antioch, one to Persia, one to India, and two remained in the dwellings of the Children of Israel summoning them to the opinion of the Messiah until most of them were killed, and the Messiah's claim was spread in east and west by the deeds of the disciples.

A., 129.—The Messiah used to say to the disciples, "I have only come from my Father and your Father to give you life from the death of ignorance, and to cure you from the disease of disobediences, and to heal you from the disease of perverse opinions and evil manners and wicked deeds, that your souls may be refined and made alive by the spirit of knowledge, and you may ascend to the kingdom of heaven beside my Father and your Father. There you will live the life of the happy ones and will be saved from the prison of the world, and the pains of the realm of existence, and the decay which is the dwelling of the miserable ones, and the neighbourhood of devils, and the dominion of Iblīs" [Satan].

A., 147.—It is related concerning Jesus, son of Mary (God's blessings and peace be upon them!) that he said, "O company of the learned, you have deviated from the way, and you have loved the world; so as kings have left wisdom to you, leave their rule to them."

A., 159.—This is the meaning of the Messiah, son of Mary (Peace be upon them!), when he had water in his right hand and bread in his left hand, "This is my father and this is my mother." He made the water father, and he made the food mother, because the water of the earth is in the place of the semen with relation to the woman. This [the earth] brings forth from this [water], and this [woman] becomes pregnant from this [semen].

A., 160.—Al Fodeil, son of 'Iyādh, said: Some people said to Jesus, son of Mary (Peace be upon him!), "By what thing do you walk upon the water?" He replied, "By faith and certainty." They said, "But we believe as you believe, and we are certain as you are certain." He said, "Then walk." When he said it they walked with him, and a wave came and raised him up, and Jesus (Peace be upon him!) said to them, "What is the matter with you?" They replied, "We feared the wave." He said, "Did you not fear the Lord of the wave?"

A., 161.—Jesus, son of Mary (Peace be upon him!) said, "Be ashamed before God (Great and glorious is He!) in your secret affairs, as you are ashamed before Him in your public affairs."

A., 165.—Verily I have seen in the Gospel of Jesus (Peace be upon him!), "From the time a dead body is placed on the bier until it is placed on the edge of the grave, God (Exalted is He!) asks of it by His greatness forty questions. First God (Exalted is He!) says, My servant, you have been pure in the sight of men for years, but you have not been pure in My sight for an hour, and every day I was looking into your heart. My servant, what were you occupied with apart from Me when you were surrounded by My blessings? Were you not deaf and unhearing?"

A., 172.—It is related that Jesus (Peace be upon him!) went out one day and met Iblīs [Satan] with honey in one hand and ashes in the other; so he said, "What are you doing, O enemy of God, with this honey and ashes?" He replied, "As regards the honey, I put it on the lips of slanderers that they may become eloquent from it; and as regards the ashes, I put them on the face of orphans that men may hate them."

Christ in Islam

A., 186.—It is mentioned concerning Jesus (Peace be upon him!) that he said, "O Lord, how can I thank Thee when my thanks is a favour from Thee for which I must give thanks?" Then God said, "When you have recognised this, you have thanked Me."

A., 197.—Jesus, son of Mary (Peace be upon them!), said, "O companies of jurists, you have sat on the road of the life to come, but you have not walked so that you might reach it, nor have you allowed anyone to pass you to it; so woe to him who is beguiled by you!"

A., 198, Cf. M., 1.—The following is related on the authority of al Sha'bī. Gabriel met Jesus (Blessing and peace be upon them!) and Jesus said to him, "When is the [last] hour?" Then Gabriel trembled in his wings and said, "He who is asked about it is no better informed than he who asks. It is burdensome in the heavens and the earth; it will only come suddenly."

A., 206.—The son of 'Adī related on the authority of Abū Sa'īd al Khadrī a tradition that when his mother handed over Jesus, son of Mary, to the school that one should teach him, the teacher said to him, "Write, *Bismillahi* (*In the name of God*)." Jesus said to him, "What is *bismi* (*In the name*)?" The teacher replied, "I do not know." Then Jesus said. "[The letter] *bā*' is *bahā*' *Allah* (*the glory*

Christ in Islam

of God), and *sīn* is *sanāuhu* (*His grandeur*), and *mīm* is *mulkuhu* (*His kingdom*), and *Allah* is the God of gods. And *ar Rahmān* (*the Merciful*) means Merciful in this world and the next; and *ar Rahīm* (*the Compassionate*) means Compassionate in the next world," etc.

[In the above passage Jesus is represented as explaining the words *Bismillahi ar Rahmān ar Rahīm* (*In the name of God, the Merciful, the Compassionate*) which occur at the beginning of all but one of the sūrahs of the Korān.]

A., 213.—God (Exalted is He!) revealed to Jesus (Peace be upon him!), "A prophet does not lack his respect except in his own country."

A., 214.—The Messiah (Peace be upon him!) said to the disciples when he gave them an injunction, and came to the end of it, "If you do what I have commanded you, you will be with me to-morrow in the kingdom of heaven with my Lord and your Lord, and you will see the angels round His throne (Exalted is He!) singing His praise and praising His holiness, and there you will enjoy all pleasures without eating and drinking."

A., 215.—Jesus (Peace be upon him!) said, "If I had said it, Thou wouldest have known it [Korān V, 116], because Thou art He who speaks in my form, and Thou art the tongue with which I speak, making it sure that Thou alone art in my desire and in my person."

Christ in Islam

A., 216.—It is related on the authority of Wahb, son of Munabbih, that Jesus, son of Mary (Peace be upon him!) said, "Woe to you, slaves of the world! What use is the spreading of the sun's light to a blind man when he does not see it? Similarly the abundance of a learned man's knowledge is of no use to him when he does not act according to it, How many fruits of trees are there, yet all of them are not useful and are not eaten! And how many learned men are there, yet all of them do not profit from what they learn! So be on your guard against the false learned men who wear woollen clothing and bend down their heads to the earth, glancing under their eyebrows as wolves glance, Their speech disagrees with their action. Who plucks grapes from thorns and figs from colocynth? Similarly the speech of a false learned man produces only falsehood. For when its owner does not tie up a camel in the desert it goes off to its home and its people; and when one who possesses knowledge does not act upon it, it departs from his breast and abandons him and leaves him void. And just as the seed is of no use without water and soil, so is faith without knowledge and works. Woe to you, slaves of the world! Everything has a sign by which it is known and witness is given to it or about it, and verily religion has three signs by which it is known: faith, knowledge, and works."

Chapter 7
Stories Connected With Jesus

A., 10.—It is related that Jesus (God's blessings and peace be upon him!) went out to pray for rain, and when [the disciples] became bored, Jesus (Peace be upon him!) said to them, "Whoever of you has committed sin, let him return." Then they all returned, and only one man remained with him in the desert. Jesus (Peace be upon him!) said to him, "Have you never committed a sin?" He replied, "By God, I am aware of nothing except that one day when I was praying a woman passed me and I looked at her with this eye; but when she passed me I put my finger in my eye, plucked it out, and threw it after the woman." Then Jesus (Peace be upon him!) said to him, "Do you pray to God, that I may say Amen to your prayer!" So he prayed and the sky was covered with clouds, and the rain poured down and they were provided with water. [Cf. A., 201, p. 121.]

A., 39.—'Omar, son of Sa'īd, said: Jesus (Peace be upon him!) passed a village, and lo! all its people were dead in the open spaces and the roads. Then he said, "O company of the

Christ in Islam

disciples, these people died because of [God's] anger, for if they had died from any other cause they would have buried one another." They said, "O Spirit of God, we should like to know what happened to them." So he asked God (Exalted is He!) and He revealed to him, "When night comes, call to them and they will answer you." When night came, he went up on a hill and called, "O people of the village!" Then one answered him, "At your service, O Spirit of God." He asked, "What is your condition, and what happened to you?" He replied, "At night we were in health and in the morning we were in hell." He said, "How did that come about?" He replied, "By our love of the world and our obedience to the people of disobediences." He said, "What kind of love had you for the world?" He replied, "The love of a boy for his mother; when it approached we rejoiced in it, and when it turned its back we grieved and wept for it." He said, "What is the matter with your companions that they have not replied to me?" He said, "Because they are bridled with bridles of fire in the hands of rough, mighty angels." He said, "Then how did you answer me from among them?" He replied, "Because I was among them but was not of them. Then when the punishment descended on them it smote me along with them, and I was suspended on the brink of Jahannam, not knowing whether I should escape from it, or be overturned into it." Then the Messiah said to the disciples, "Verily the eating of barley bread with pounded salt, and the wearing of sackcloth, and sleeping on dunghills often accompanies health in this world and the next."

A., 54.—The following is related on the authority of Jarīr, on the authority of Laith. A man accompanied Jesus, son of Mary (Peace be upon him!), and said, "I will be with you and will accompany you." So they set off and came to the bank of a river and sat down to breakfast; and they had three loaves. They ate two loaves, and a third loaf was left over. Then Jesus (Peace be upon him!) rose up and went to the river and drank, after which he returned, but did not find the loaf; so he said to the man, "Who took the loaf?" He replied, "I do not know." Then he set off with his companion and saw a gazelle with two of her young. The narrator says, He called one of them and it came to him; then he cut its throat and roasted part of it, and he and that man ate. Then he said to the young gazelle, "Rise, by the permission of God." When it rose and went away, he said to the man, "I ask you by Him who has shown you this sign, Who took the loaf?" He replied, "I do not know." Afterwards they came to a wadi with water in it and Jesus took the man's hand and they walked on the water. Then when

Christ in Islam

they had crossed he said to him, "I ask you by Him who has shown you this sign, Who took the loaf?" He replied, "I do not know." Then they came to a desert and sat down, and Jesus (Peace be upon him!) began to collect earth and a heap of sand, after which he said, "Become gold, by the permission of God (Exalted is He!)." It became gold, and he divided it into three parts and said, "A third is for me, a third for you, and a third for him who took the loaf." Then he said, "I am the one who took the loaf." He said, "It is all yours." Jesus (Peace be upon him!) then left him and two men came to him in the desert while he had the wealth with him and wished to take it from him and kill him. He said, "It is among us in thirds; so send one of you to the village to buy food for us to eat." The narrator said: They sent one of them, and he who was sent said [to himself], "Why should I divide this wealth with these men? I shall put poison in this food and kill them and take the wealth myself." So he did so. And these two men said, "Why should we give this man a third of the wealth? When he returns we shall kill him, and divide the wealth between us." The narrator said: So when he returned they killed him and ate the food and died; and that wealth remained in the desert with those three men lying dead beside it. Then Jesus (Peace be upon him!)

Christ in Islam

passed them in that condition and said to his companions, "This is the world; so beware of it."

[In Asin's collection this is followed by three variations of the same story.]

A., 67; *M.*, 59.—It is related that a robber had been committing highway robbery among the Children of Israel for forty years. [One day] Jesus (Peace be upon him!) passed by followed by a pious man of the Children of Israel who was one of the disciples. Then the robber said to himself, "This is the prophet of God who is passing with his disciple beside him; if I went down, I should make a third with them." So he went down and began to make to approach the disciple, but he was despising himself out of respect for the disciple, and saying to himself, "The like of me cannot walk beside this pious man." [The narrator] said: The disciple noticed him and said to himself, "This man is walking beside me." So he drew himself together and went to Jesus (Blessing and peace be upon him!) and walked beside him, and the robber remained behind him. Then God (Exalted is He!) revealed to Jesus (Blessing and peace be upon him!), "Tell them to begin their works afresh, for I have nullified their past works. As regards the disciple, I have nullified his good deeds because of his self-conceit; and as regards the other, I have nullified his evil deeds because he despised himself." So [Jesus] informed them about that, and joined the robber to himself in his wandering and made him one of his disciples. [Cf. *A.*, 137, p. 109.]

A., 84.—It is related that Jesus (Peace be upon him!) passed three people whose bodies were wasted and who were pale and said, "What has brought on you that which I see?" They replied, "Fear of hell." He said, "It is God's duty to render secure him who fears." Afterwards he passed from them and came to other three, and lo! they were in greater emaciation and paleness, so he said, "What has brought on you that which I see?" They replied, "Desire of Paradise." He said, "It is God's duty to give you what you hope for." After that he passed from them and came to other three, and lo! they were in still greater emaciation and paleness as though mirrors of light were over their faces, so he said, "What has brought on you that which I see?" They replied, "We love God (Great and glorious is He!)." He said, "You are those who are nearest to God; you are those who are nearest to God; you are those who are nearest to God."

[This is followed in Asin's collection by a variant of the same story.]

A., 84 *ter.*—It has reached us that Jesus, son of Mary (Peace be upon him!), passed four hundred thousand women who looked pale and who were wearing tunics of hair and wool. Jesus

Christ in Islam

(Peace be upon him!) said, "What has made you pale, O companies of women?" They replied, "The thought of hell has made us pale, O son of Mary; he who enters hell will not taste cold or drink."

A., 88; *M.*, 67.—It is related that Jesus (Peace be upon him!) passed a man who was blind, leprous, lame, paralysed on both sides, whose flesh was falling from elephantiasis, but who was saying, "Praise be to God who has kept me free from that with which He has afflicted many of His creatures!" Then Jesus said, "O man, what affliction do I see removed from you?" He replied, "O Spirit of God, I am better than he in whose heart God has not put the knowledge of Himself which He has put in my heart." He said to him, "You have spoken the truth; give me your hand." He gave him his hand, and lo! he became the most beautiful of men in face and the finest in figure, for God had removed from him what he was suffering from. So he accompanied Jesus (Peace be upon him!) and worshipped with him.

A., 99.—It is said that while Jesus (Peace be upon him!) was sitting and an old man was working with a spade with which he was stirring up the ground, Jesus said, "O God, take away hope from him." Then the old man put away the spade and lay down and remained for a time. Jesus then said, "O God, restore hope to him," and he got up and began to work. Jesus asked him about that and he said, "While I was working, lo! my soul said to me, 'How long are you going to work, for you are a very old man?' So I threw away the spade and lay down. Then my soul said to me, 'By God, you must have food as long as you remain;' so I arose to my spade."

A., 102; *M.*, 77.—It is related that Jesus (Peace be upon him!) passed by a skull and kicked it with his foot and said, "Speak, by the permission of God." It said, "O Spirit of God, I was a king at such and such a time. While I was sitting in my kingdom on my throne of state with my crown on my head and my troops and my suite around me, lo! the angel of death appeared to me. Then every limb of mine perished when he appeared, and my soul went out to him. So would that there had been abandonment with respect to those companies! And would that there had been solitude with respect to that society!"

[This is followed in Asin's collection by four other accounts of the story of the skull. The following is the fourth and longest of them.]

A., 102 *quinquies*.—The story of the skull. It is mentioned, but God knows best, that Jesus (Peace be upon him!) one day passed a wadi called the Wadi of the Resurrection, and lo! he saw a white skull whose bones were crumbling. Its whiteness astonished him, for its owner had

Christ in Islam

been dead for seventy-two years; so Jesus (Peace be upon him!) said, "O God, whom eye cannot see, or opinions disorder, or men describe, I ask Thee to permit this skull to tell me to what people it belonged." God revealed to him, "O Jesus, speak to it and it will speak to you by My power, for I am omnipotent." [The narrator] said: Then Jesus performed his ablutions, and having prayed two rek'as, approached it and said, "In the name of God, the Merciful, the Compassionate." Then the skull answered him with ready tongue, and it was saying, "O Spirit of God, you have named the best of the names." Jesus (Peace be upon him!) said to it, "I ask you by the mighty God, will you not tell me where are the beauty and the whiteness, and where are the flesh and the fat, and where are the bones and the spirit?" Then it replied to him, "O Spirit of God, as regards the beauty and the whiteness, the dust has changed them; and as regards the flesh and the fat, the worms have eaten them; and as regards the bones, they have crumbled; and as regards the spirit, it is to-day in hell in severe punishment." Jesus (Peace be upon him!) said to it, "I ask you by the mighty God, to what people did you belong?" It replied to him, "O Spirit of God, I belonged to a people with whom God was angry in the world." He asked it, "How was God angry with you in the world?" It replied to him, "O Spirit

Christ in Islam

of God, God sent us a prophet who brought us the truth, but we rejected him, and who commanded us to obey God, but we disobeyed Him; so God sent down on us rain and thunderbolts for seven years and seven months and seven days. Then one day some of the avenging angels alighted upon us, every one of whom had two whips, one of iron and one of fire; and an angel kept grasping my soul from joint to joint, and from vein to vein, till the soul reached the windpipe." The skull said: "After that the angel of death stretched out his hand and took out my soul." Jesus (Peace be upon him!) said to it, "I ask you by the mighty God, will you not describe to me the angel of death?" It replied to him, "O Spirit of God, he has a hand in the East and a hand in the West; his head is in the top of the seventh heaven and his feet are in the lowest borders of the seven [lit. seventh] earths; the world is between his knees and created things are before him." It continued, "O apostle of God, only an hour later two black and blue angels came to me with voices like resounding thunder and eyes like swift lightning and short, curly hair, who were piercing the earth with their nails. Then they asked me, 'Who is your Lord, and who is your prophet, and who is your imām?' [leader in theology]. I was terrified at them, O Spirit of God, and said to them, 'I have no Lord, or prophet, or imām but God.' They said to me, 'You are lying, O enemy of God and of your soul;' and gave me a terrible blow with a sledgehammer of iron, from the violence of which blow I felt my bones were broken and my chin rent; and they threw me into the depths of Jahannam where they punished me as God wills. While I was in that condition the two recording angels who write down what people do in the world came and said to me, 'O enemy of God, journey with us to the dwellings of the people of Paradise.'" It continued, "So I journeyed with them to the first of the gates of Paradise, and lo! Paradise had eight gates made of bricks of gold and silver; its earth is musk, its grass is saffron, its stones are pearls and jacinths, its rivers are milk and water and honey, its inhabitants have the neighbouring planets as friends restricted in tents,[1] the work of Him who possesses glory and honour. I rejoiced in it, O Spirit of God; then they said to me, 'O enemy of God and of yourself, you did not do good in the world that this might be yours; but journey with us to the dwellings of the people of hell.'" It went on, "Then I journeyed with them to the first of the gates of hell in which snakes and scorpions were whistling, and I asked them 'For whom is this punishment?' They replied to me, 'For you and for those who devour

---

[1] The text at this point is not clear; the translation of this phrase is therefore a conjecture.—JR

the property of orphans by oppression.'" It continued, "Thereafter I journeyed with them to the second gate and lo! there were men suspended by their beards like dogs, with blood and pus before them for food. I asked them [the angels], 'For whom is this punishment?' They replied to me, 'For you, and for those who drink wine in the world and eat what is forbidden.'" It continued, "I then journeyed with them to the third gate, and lo! there were men with fire entering their mouths and coming out at their backs. I asked, 'For whom is this punishment?' They replied to me, 'For you, and for those who reproach virtuous women in the world.'" It went on, "I journeyed next with them to the fourth gate, and lo! there were Women hanging by their tongues with fire coming out of their mouths. I asked them [the angels], 'For whom is this punishment?' They replied to me, 'For you, and for those who neglect prayer in the world.'" It continued, "Afterwards I journeyed with them to the fifth gate, and lo! there were women suspended by their hair with fire above them. I asked them [the angels], 'For whom is this punishment?' They replied to me, 'For you, and for those who adorn themselves in the world for people who are not their spouses.'" It continued, "Then I journeyed with them to the sixth gate, and lo! there were women suspended by their hair and their mouths. I asked them [the angels], 'For whom is this punishment?' They replied to me, 'For you, and for the women who go astray in the world.'" It went on, "Thereafter I journeyed with them to the seventh gate, and lo! there were men under whom was a well called Hell's Well into which I was thrown, O Spirit of God, and in which I have endured fierce punishment and seen many terrible things." Then Jesus (Peace be Upon him!) said, "O skull, if you wish, ask me for something, by the permission of God." It said, "O Spirit of God, pray God for me to send me back to the world." So he prayed to God for it, and He brought it to life for him and sent it back for him sound by the power of God (Praise be to Him!). It remained for twelve years worshipping God along with Jesus (Peace be Upon him!) until the inevitable, i.e. death, came to it. It then died in faith, and God in His mercy made it one of the people of Paradise.

A., 106.—It is related concerning Jesus (Peace be upon him!) that he came on a fire which was kindled over a man in the desert. Jesus then took water to put it out, and the fire changed into a youth, and the man changed into fire. So Jesus (Peace be upon him!) wept and said, "O Lord, restore them to their former state that I may see what their sin was." Then that fire was removed from them, and lo! they were a man and a youth. The man said, "O Jesus,

Christ in Islam

I have been afflicted in the world by love of this youth, and desire urged me on until I sinned with him one Thursday night, after which I sinned with him another day. Then a man came upon us and said to us, 'Woe to you! Fear God!' I replied to him, 'I am not afraid, and I do not fear.' Then when I died, and the youth died, God (Great and glorious is He!) turned us into what you see. Sometimes he becomes fire and burns me, and sometimes I become fire and burn him. And this is our punishment until the Day of Resurrection."

A., 120.—In one of the books which have been translated [it is said] that John and Simon were among the disciples. John never sat in any company without laughing and making those around him laugh; and Simon never sat in any company without weeping and making those around him weep. [Once] Simon said to John, "How often you laugh, as though you had ceased from your work!" John replied to him, "How often you weep, as though you had despaired of your Lord!" Then God revealed to the Messiah, "The more attractive of the two natures to Me is John's nature."

A., 121.—In a book also [it is said] that Jesus, son of Mary, met John, son of Zechariah (Blessing and peace be upon them!) and John smiled to him. Then Jesus said to him, "Verily you smile the smile of a believer." John said to him, "Verily you frown the frown of a despondent one." God then revealed to Jesus, "What John does is more attractive to me."

[While the two preceding passages presumably come from the same source, it should be noted that in the Arabic there is no confusion between the two Johns. In 120 the name is Yuhannā, and in 121 it is Yahyā.]

A., 131.—It is mentioned that Jesus (Peace be upon him!) used to raise the dead to life by the permission of God (Exalted is He!). Some unbelievers [once] said to him, "You have raised people who have died recently, and perhaps they were not dead; so raise for us one who died in the earliest times." He said to them, "Choose whom you will." They said, "Raise for us Shem, son of Noah." Then he came to his grave and prayed two rek'as and called on God (Exalted is He!), and God raised Shem, son of Noah, and lo! his head and beard had become white. But someone said, "What is this? There were no white hairs in your day." He replied, "I heard the summons, and I thought the Resurrection had come, so the hair of my head and beard became white from terror." Someone asked, "How long have you been dead?" He replied, "For four thousand years; but the agony of death has not left me yet."

A., 137.—In the time of Jesus (Blessing and peace be upon him!) there was a man called Accursed for his avarice. One day a man who

Christ in Islam

wished to make a raid came to him and said, "O Accursed, give me some arms to help me in my raid, and by so doing you will be safe from hell"; but he turned away from him and gave him nothing. The man then turned back, but the accursed one repented and called to him and gave him his sword. The man returned, and Jesus (Peace be upon him!), accompanied by a pious man who had worshipped God for seventy years, met him and said to him, "Where have you come from with this sword?" He replied, "The accursed one gave me it." So Jesus rejoiced at his almsgiving. The accursed one was [one day] sitting at his door, and when Jesus (Peace be upon him!) passed him accompanied by the pious man, the accursed one said to himself, "I will arise and look at the face of Jesus and at the face of the pious man." So when he arose and looked at them the pious man said, "I shall fly and run from this accursed one before he burns me with his fire." Then God (Great and glorious is He!) revealed to Jesus (Peace be upon him!), "Say to My servant, I have forgiven this sinner because of his almsgiving with the sword and because of his love for you; and say to the pious man, Verily he will be your friend in Paradise." The pious man said, "By God, I do not wish Paradise in his company, neither do I wish a friend like him." So God (Great and glorious is He!) revealed to Jesus

Christ in Islam

(Peace be upon him!), "Say to My servant, Verily you were not pleased with My decree and you despised My servant, so I have made you accursed among the people of hell; I have changed your abodes in Paradise for his in hell, and have given your abodes in Paradise to My servant and his abodes in hell to you." [Cf. *A*., 67; *M*., 59, p. 99 ?].

A., 138.—'Abdallah, son of Habān, al Bokhārī told us on the authority of Abū al Faraj al Azdī that Jesus, son of Mary (Peace be upon them!), passed by a village in which was a fuller. The people of the village said, "O Jesus, verily this fuller tears our clothes for us and keeps them; so pray to God that He should not let him come back with his bundle." So Jesus (Peace be upon him!) said, "O God, do not let him come back with his bundle." [The narrator] said: Then the fuller went away to clean the clothes, and he had three loaves with him. And one who was practising devotion in those hills came to the fuller and said to him, "Have you any bread to give me to eat, or to show me that I may smell its odour? For I have not eaten any bread for such and such a time." So he gave him a loaf, and he said, "O fuller, God forgive you your sin and purify your heart!" Then he gave him the second, and he said, "O fuller, God forgive you your past and your future sins!" So he gave him the third to eat, and he said,

Christ in Islam

"O fuller, God build you a palace in Paradise!" The fuller returned safe in the evening and the villagers said, "O Jesus, this fuller has come back." He said, "Call him." Then when he came to him he said, "O fuller, tell me what you did to-day." He replied, "One of the pilgrims of those hills came to me asking for food and I gave him three loaves to eat, and with every loaf I gave him he offered up prayers for me." Jesus (Blessing and Peace be upon him!) said, "Bring your bundle that I may look at it." He gave him it and he opened it, and lo! there was in it a black snake curbed with an iron curb. Jesus (Peace be upon him!) said, "O black one!" It replied, "At your service, O prophet of God!" He said, "Have you not been sent to this man?" It replied, "Yes, but a pilgrim from those hills came to him and asked him for food, and with every loaf he gave him to eat he offered up a prayer for him, and an angel was standing and saying 'Amen!' Then God (Exalted is He!) sent an angel to me and he curbed me with an iron curb." Then Jesus (Peace be upon him!) said, "O fuller, recommence your work, for God has forgiven you by the blessing of your almsgiving to Him." [Cf. A., 210, p. 126.]

A., 143 bis.—The prophet—i.e. Mohammad—(God bless him and grant him peace!) said that God commanded John, son of Zechariah, five words according to which he was to act, and he

Christ in Islam

was to command the Children of Israel that they should act according to them, but he was on the point of delaying with them. So Jesus said, "Verily God has commanded you five words according to which you should act, and you must command the Children of Israel that they should act according to them; so either you must command them, or I will command them." John said, "I am afraid that if you precede me with them, I may be swallowed up or punished." Then he gathered the people tagether in Jerusalem, and the mosque was full and they sat on the pinnacles; and he said, "Verily God commanded me five words according to which I should act and should order you to act according to them. The first is that you should worship God and associate nothing with Him; for he who associates anything with God is like a man who buys a slave with all his property, in gold or documents, and says, 'This is my house and this is my work, so work and bring me profit,' then he works and brings profit for someone else. So which of you wishes to be like that? And verily God commands you to practise prayer; and when you pray, do not turn about, for God directs His face to His servant's face in his prayer so long as he does not turn about. And He commands you to observe fasting, for that is like a man in a company who has a purse in which is musk whose perfume pleases them all, or pleases him; and verily the perfume of him who fasts is better in God's estimation than the perfume of musk. And He commands you to give alms; for that is like a man whom the enemy have taken captive and bound his hand to his neck and put him forward to execute him [lit. to strike his neck], who says, 'I will ransom it [his neck] from you by little or by much;' so he ransoms himself from them. And He commands you to glorify God; for that is like a man in pursuit of whom the enemy go out in haste until he comes to a strong fort and preserves himself from them. Similarly the worshipper preserves himself from the devil only by glorifying God."

[Although this is attributed to John the Baptist, it is included because Jesus is said to have been prepared to say it if John did not.]

A., 148.—It is related in the record that Jesus (Blessing and peace be upon him!) passed a village; and in that village there was a hill, and in the hill there was great weeping and wailing. He said to the villagers, "What is this weeping and this wailing in this hill?" They replied, "O Jesus, from the time we settled in this village we have been hearing this weeping and this wailing in this hill." Then Jesus (Peace be upon him!) said, "O Lord, permit this hill to speak to me." God gave the hill utterance and it said, "O Jesus, what do you want from me?" He said, "Tell me the meaning of your weeping and wailing." It said, "O Jesus, I am the hill from which the idols were being hewn which men worship instead of God, and I am afraid lest God (Exalted is He!) should cast me into the fire of Jahannam, for I heard God saying, 'Fear hell whose fuel is men and stones.'" [Korān II, 22; LXVI, 6.] Then God revealed to Jesus (Blessing and peace be upon him!), "Say to the him, Be at peace, for I have protected it from Jahannam."

A., 151.—Jesus, son of Mary (Peace be upon them!), passed a graveyard and called to a man in it. Then God (Exalted is He!) brought him to life, and [Jesus] said, "Who are you?" He replied, "I was a carrier, carrying things for people. One day I carried some firewood for a man and broke off a piece of it with which I was pierced; and I am being sued for it since my death."

A., 152.—It is related that Jesus (Blessing and peace be upon him!) passed a grave and kicked it with his foot and said, "O you who are in the grave, arise by the permission of God (Exalted is He!)." Then a man arose from the grave and said, "O Spirit of God, what do you want with me? For I have been standing in judgment for seventy years till I heard the shout, 'Answer the Spirit of God.'" Jesus said, "O you, you have committed many faults and sins, so what did you do?" He replied, "O Spirit of God, was a seller of fuel who carried firewood on my head and ate what was allowable and gave alms." Jesus said, "Praise be to God! A seller of fuel who carried firewood on his head and ate what was allowable and gave alms, and he has been standing in judgment for seventy years!" Then Jesus asked him about what his Lord said to him in the judgment, and he said, "O Spirit of God, one of the rebukes of my Lord was that He said, 'Do you remember the day My servant, so and so, hired you to carry a bundle of firewood for him, and you took a piece of wood from it and were pierced with it and threw it away from its place in the bundle out of your despite for Me, although you knew that I am God who looks at your work and your intention?'"

A., 164.—It is related on the authority of Mohammad, son of Abū Mūsā, concerning Jesus, son of Mary (Peace be upon him!), that he passed an afflicted man and treated him kindly and said, "O God, I beseech Thee to heal him." Then God (Exalted is He!) revealed to him, "How can I heal him from that with which I am healing him?" [Showing that bodily trouble may lead to spiritual advantage.]

A., 170.—Jesus (Peace be upon him!) passed a young man watering a garden, and the young man said to Jesus, "Ask your Lord to provide me with an atom of His love." Jesus replied, "You are not able for an atom." So he said,

Christ in Islam

"Half an atom." Then Jesus (Peace be upon him!) said, "O Lord, provide him with half an atom of Thy love;" after which Jesus (Peace be upon him!) went away. A long time afterwards, when he passed that young man's place, he asked about him and the people said, "He became possessed and went to the mountains." Then Jesus (Peace be upon him!) prayed God to show him to him, and he saw him among the mountains and found him standing on a high rock whose tip reached to the sky. Jesus (Peace be upon him!) saluted him, but he did not return the salutation; so he said, "I am Jesus." Then God (Exalted is He!) revealed to Jesus, "How can he in whose heart is half an atom of My love listen to the words of men? By My might and glory, if I were to cleave him with a saw, he would not be aware of that!" [Cf. *A.*, 189, p. 120.]

A., 171.—It is related in the stories that John [the Baptist] and Jesus (Peace be upon them!) were walking in the market when a woman knocked against them. Then John said, "I am not cognisant of that." Jesus said, "Praise be to God! Your body is with me, but where is your heart?" He replied, "O cousin, if my heart found rest in something other than God for the twinkling of an eye, I should think that I had not known God."

A., 178.—Wahb, son of Munabbih, said: Jesus, son of Mary (Peace be upon him!), went out one day with a company of his companions and when the day was advanced they passed a field where the corn was ready to be rubbed, and they said, "O prophet of God, verily we are hungry." Then God revealed to him, "Give them permission concerning their food." So he gave them permission, and they separated in the field rubbing and eating. But while they were doing that, the owner of the field came, and he was saying, "It is my field and my land which I inherited from my ancestors. By whose permission are you eating, you people?" [The narrator] said: Then Jesus prayed to his Lord, and God (Exalted is He!) raised up all who had possessed that land from the time of Adam till that time. Then lo! beside every ear, or what God wills, was a man or woman, all of them shouting, "It is my field and my land which I inherited from my ancestors." The man was terrified at them—and word of Jesus (Peace be upon him!) had reached him, but he had not recognised him—so when he recognised him, he said, "I apologise to you, O apostle of God. My field and my possessions are at your disposal." Then Jesus (Peace be upon him!) wept and said, "Woe to you! All these have inherited this land and have peopled it, then have gone away from it; and you too will go away from it, and overtaking them, will have no land or possessions."

A., 179.—Mālik, son of Anas, said: It reached

me that two women came to Jesus (Peace be upon him!) and said, "O Spirit of God, pray to God for us to bring forth our father for us, for he perished and we are absent from him." He said, "Do you know his grave?" They replied, "Yes." So he went with them, and they came to a grave and said, "This is it." Then he prayed to God and one was brought forth to them, but lo! it was not he; so he prayed and he was sent back. Then they led him to another grave and he prayed that he should be brought forth, and he came forth, and lo! it was he. They clung to him and saluted him and said, "O prophet of God, O teacher of good, pray God to make him stay with us." He said, "How can I pray for him when no provision by which he may live has been left for him?" Then he sent him back and departed.

A., 151.—Mālik, son of Anas, said: It reached me that Jesus (Peace be upon him!) came to a village whose fortresses had fallen in ruins, whose streams were dried up, and whose trees were blighted. Then he called, "O ruin, where are your people?" But no one answered him. Again he called, "O ruin, where are your people?" But no one answered him. Then a voice cried, "Jesus, son of Mary, they perished and the earth swallowed them up, and their works returned as chains on their necks till the Day of Resurrection." So Jesus (Peace be upon him!) wept.

Christ in Islam

A., 183.—Joseph, son of Asbāt, said: One of the disciples died and they grieved bitterly for him and complained of that to the Messiah (God bless him and grant him peace!). Then he stood over his grave and prayed, and God (Exalted is He!) brought him back to life; and he had on his feet sandals of fire. Jesus asked about that and he said, "By God, I was never disobedient, except that [once] I passed one who was wronged and did not help him, so I was shod with these sandals."

A., 189.—It is related that Jesus (Peace be upon him!) one day passed a hill in which he saw a cell. He drew near it and found in it a devotee whose back was bent, whoge body was wasted, and in whom austerity had reached its utmost limits. Jesus saluted him and wondered at his evidences [of devotion] which he saw. So Jesus said to him, "How long have you been in this place?" He replied, "For seventy years I have been asking Him for one thing which He has not granted me yet. Perhaps you, O Spirit of God, may intercede for me concerning it, then possibly it may be granted." Jesus said, "What is your requirement?" He replied, "I asked Him to let me taste the amount of an atom of His pure love." Jesus said to him, "I shall pray to God for you about that." So he prayed for him that night, and God (Exalted is He!) revealed to him, "I have accepted your

Christ in Islam

intercession and granted your request." Jesus (Peace be upon him!) returned to him to the place after some days to see what the condition of the devotee was, and saw the cell had fallen down and a great fissure had appeared in the ground below it. Jesus (Peace be upon him!) went down into that fissure and went some leagues in it and saw the devotee in a cave under that him standing with his eyes staring and his mouth open. Then Jesus (Peace be upon him!) saluted him, but he did not give him an answer. While Jesus was wondering at his condition someone shouted to him, "O Jesus, he has asked us for something like an atom of Our pure love, and We knew that he was not able for that, so We gave him a seventieth part of an atom, and he is bewildered in it thus; so what would it have been like if We had given him more than that?" [Cf. *A.*, 170, p. 116.]

A., 201.—It is related that Jesus, son of Mary, (Peace be upon him!) went out with the people to pray for rain; and God revealed to him, "Do not ask for rain while sinners are with you." Jesus told them of that and shouted among them, "Let him among us who belongs to those who have committed faults and sins depart." The narrator said: All the people departed except one man who had something wrong with his right eye. Jesus (Peace be upon him!) said to him, "Why did you not depart with the people?"

Christ in Islam

He replied, "O Spirit of God, I have never disobeyed God with the glance of an eye; but [once] I turned and looked unintentionally with this eye at a woman's foot, so I plucked it out; and if I had looked with the other eye, I would have plucked it out." [The narrator] said: Then Jesus (Peace be upon him!) wept till his beard became wet with his tears, and said to him, "Do you pray to God for us!" He said, "God forbid that I should pray, when you are God's Spirit and Word!" Then Jesus (Peace be upon him!) raised his hands and said, "O God, verily Thou hast created us and hast stood security for our provisions; so send the sky raining copiously upon us." Jesus (Peace be upon him!) had not finished his prayer before the rain descended and covered the worshippers and the country. [Cf. A., 10, p. 95.]

A., 202.—It is related that John [the Baptist] and Jesus (Blessing and peace be upon them!) went together on a journey, and John (Peace be upon him!) once slept during worship which Jesus (Peace be upon him!) performed. Jesus (Peace be upon him!) wished to waken him, but God (Exalted is He!) revealed to Jesus (Blessing and peace be upon him!), "O Jesus, verily John's spirit is with Me in My holy presence and his body is before Me in My earth; and I have made him excel in beauty the noble ones of My angels."

Christ in Islam

A., 203.—The historians and biographers mentioned that a man called Isaac, belonging to the Children of Israel, in the time of Jesus, son of Mary (Peace be upon them!), had a cousin who was one of the most beautiful people of her time to whom he was devoted. She died, and he attached himself to her grave and remained for a time visiting her regularly. One day Jesus passed him when he was weeping at her grave, and Jesus (Peace be upon him!) said to him, "What is making you weep, Isaac?" He replied, "O Spirit of God, I had a cousin who was my wife, whom I loved ardently; but she has died and this is her grave, and I am unable to be patient without her, for separation from her has killed me." Jesus said to him, "Would you like me to bring her to life for you by God's permission?" He said, "Yes, O Spirit of God." So Jesus stood over the grave and said, "Arise, you who are in this grave, by God's permission." Then the grave burst open and a black slave came out of it with fire issuing from his nostrils and eyes and the other openings of his face, and he was saying, "There is no God but God. Jesus is God's Spirit and Word, His servant and His apostle." Isaac said, "O Spirit and Word of God, this grave is not the one in which my wife is, this is it;" and he pointed to another grave. So Jesus said to the black one, "Return to the condition in which you were." He fell down dead and he hid him in his grave. Thereafter he stood over the other grave and said, "Arise, you who are dwelling in this grave, by God's permission." Then the woman arose, and she was scattering the dust from her face. Jesus said, "Is this your wife?" He replied, "Yes, O Spirit of God." He said, "Take her by the hand and go away." He took her and went off, but he became sleepy and said to her, "Watchfulness at your grave has killed me, so I want to take some rest." She said, "Do so." Then he put his head in her lap and slept. While he was sleeping the king's son passed her; he was beautiful and good-looking, with lordly mien, and was riding on a fine horse. When she saw him she fell in love with him and rose up quickly to him; and when he saw her she affected his heart. Then she came to him and said, "Take me;" so he took her up behind him on his horse and went on. When her husband arose and looked and did not see her, he arose to search for her. He followed the traces of the horse and overtook them and said to the king's son, "Give me my wife who is my cousin." But she denied him and said, "I am the slavegirl of the king's son." He said, "No, you are my wife and my cousin." She said, "I do not know you; I am only the slavegirl of the king's son." Then the king's son said to him, "Do you want to corrupt my slavegirl?" He said, "By God, she is my wife, and Jesus, son of Mary, raised her for me

Christ in Islam

by God's permission after she had been dead." While they were disputing, Jesus (God bless him and grant him peace!) passed, and Isaac said, "O Spirit of God, is not this my wife whom you brought to life for me by God's permission?" He said, "Yes." She said, "O Spirit of God, he is lying, for I am the slavegirl of the king's son." And the king's son said, "This is my slavegirl." Jesus said, "Are you not she whom I raised to life by God's permission?" She said, "No, by God, O Spirit of God." He said, "Then restore to us what we gave you;" and she fell down dead. Then Jesus said, "Whoever wishes to look at a man whom God caused to die while he was an unbeliever, then brought him to life and caused him to die a Muslim, let him look at that black one; and whoever wishes to look at a woman whom God caused to die while she was a believer, then brought her to life and caused her to die an unbeliever, let him look at this woman." And Isaac, the Israelite, covenanted with God (Exalted is He!) that he would never marry; and he wandered aimlessly like a madman in the deserts, weeping.

A., 208.—I saw in a book that Jesus (Blessing and peace be upon him!) passed a man who was making donkey-saddles and saying in his worship, "O Lord, if I knew where Thine ass is on which Thou ridest, I would make a saddle for it and inlay it with jewels." Then the Messiah shook him and said, "Woe to you! Has God (Exalted is He!) an ass?" Then God (Exalted is He!) revealed to Jesus (Blessing and peace be upon him!), "Leave the man alone, for he has glorified Me according to his ability."

A., 210.—It is related that some people passed Jesus, son of Mary, and he said, "One of these will die to-day, if God will." Then they went away. In the evening they returned to him with bundles of firewood, and he said, "Put them down." Then he said to him of whom he said that he would die that day, "Loosen your firewood." He loosened it, and lo! there was a black snake in it. Jesus said, "What have you done to-day?" He replied, "I have done nothing." He said, "Consider what you have done." He said, "I have done nothing, except that I had a piece of bread in my hand, and a poor man passed me and begged from me and I gave him some of it." Then he said, "By it [death] was averted from you." [Cf. A., 138, p. 111.]

The following saying about Jesus is attributed to Mohammad.

A., 211.—Verily God (Exalted is He!) has sent me out of mercy to all men. Summon [them] in my name (God have mercy on you!) and do not disagree as the disciples disagreed with Jesus, for he summoned them to do something similar to that to which I summon you, and those who were in his vicinity believed. It displeased him, and Jesus, son of Mary, complained of that to God; and in the morning every man of them was speaking the language of the people to which he went. Then Jesus said to them, "This is a matter upon which God is resolved for you; so go and accomplish it."

A., 222.—It is related that Jesus (Peace be upon him!) one day passed a man standing between two graves, who was bowing and worshipping. He saluted him and said, "I see you between these two bowing and worshipping." He replied to him, "They are my parents who were kind and gentle to me; so when they died I took an oath on myself that I would worship God between their graves till I died." He asked him, "How long, sir, have you been doing this?" He replied, "Three hundred years." He said, "Has any news come to you from God (Exalted is He!) that He has forgiven you, or have you any request to Him, or have you prayed to Him about anything?" He replied, "No news has come to me; but I have had a request to Him: I prayed to Him that He should let me meet Jesus, but I do not know whether He has accepted my prayer or not." Then Jesus said to him, "Be of good cheer; He has accepted your prayer. I am Jesus." He said to him, "O Jesus, by Him who has accepted my prayer, would you not stretch out your leg that I might place my head on it for an hour?" So Jesus (Peace be upon him!) stretched out his leg, and he put his head on it and lifted up his eyes to heaven and said, "O God, by the honour of this prophet with Thee, as Thou hast accepted my prayer and caused me to meet him, I beseech Thee to take my spirit in his bosom." He had not come to the end of his prayer before he died with his head in the lap of Jesus (Peace be upon him!). Then Jesus looked for something in which to shroud him, but found nothing for him except his worn cloak and a brick which he used to use when he wished to sleep. So Jesus said, "O Lord, when Thou hast gathered the first ones and the last ones, and askest them about what they have gained, about what wilt Thou ask this servant?" Then God revealed to him, "O Jesus, by My greatness and My majesty, I will ask him about this cloak, whence he acquired it, and about this brick, from what ground he made it, or from what wall he took it. Verily I have sworn by Myself, if an oppressor comes near Me, I will be an oppressor. By My greatness and My majesty, I will make him who mixes water with bricks separate the water from the bricks." Then Jesus prayed, "O God, forgive us by Thy mercy, and favour us with Thy kindness and Thy Paradise; and pardon us all and make us die Muslims and join us to the upright. And praise be to God, the Lord of the worlds!"

www.ingramcontent.com/pod-product-compliance
Lightning Source LLC
Chambersburg PA
CBHW031254290426
44109CB00012B/573